P9-DBI-240

LANDSCAPING
WITH
PERENNIALS

LANDSCAPING WITH PERENNIALS

Series Concept: Robert J. Dolezal
Encyclopedia Concept: Barbara K. Dolezal
Managing Editor: Jill Fox
Encyclopedia Writer: Elizabeth Rhein
Perennials Gardening Consultant: J. Malcolm Hillan
Photography Editor: John M. Rickard
Designer: Jerry Simon
Layout: Rik Boyd
Photoshop Artist: Gerald A. Bates
Horticulturist: Peggy Henry
Photo Stylist: Peggy Henry
Copy Editor: Barbara Coster
Proofreaders: Jane Merryman, Ken DellaPenta
Index: Aubrey McClellan, ALTA Indexing

Copyright © 2001
Creative Publishing international, Inc.
5900 Green Oak Drive
Minnetonka, MN 55343
1-800-328-3895
All rights reserved
Printed in U.S.A. by Quebecor World
10 9 8 7 6 5 4 3 2 1

President/CEO: David D. Murphy
Vice President/Editorial: Patricia K. Jacobsen
Vice President/Retail Sales & Marketing: Richard M. Miller

Home Improvement/*Gardening*
Executive Editor: Bryan Trandem
Editorial Director: Jerri Farris
Creative Director: Tim Himsel

Created by: Dolezal & Associates,
in partnership with Creative Publishing international, Inc.,
in cooperation with Black & Decker.
BLACK&DECKER. is a trademark of the Black & Decker
Corporation and is used under license.

Library of Congress Cataloging-in-Publication Data

Finley, Elizabeth Navas.
  Landscaping with perennials : flowering plants & shrubs for home
gardens / author, Elizabeth Navas Finley ; photographer, John Rickard.
    p. cm. -- (Black & Decker outdoor home)
  ISBN 0-86573-459-3 (hardcover) -- ISBN 0-86573-460-7 (softcover)
  1. Perennials. 2. Landscape gardneing. I. Rickard, John M. II.
Title. III. Series.
  SB434 .R49 2000
  635.9'32--dc21
                                        00-048503

ISBN 0–86573–459–3 (hardcover)
ISBN 0–86573–460–7 (softcover)

PHOTOGRAPHY & ILLUSTRATION

PRINCIPAL PHOTOGRAPHY

JOHN M. RICKARD: pgs. *iv (top, 2nd from top, 3rd from top), v, vi, vii, viii,* 2, 3, 4 (mid L), 6, 7, 8 (top L & bot), 9, 10, 12, 13, 14 (bot L), 15 (bot), 16, 17, 18, 19, 20, 21, 24 (mid R), 25, 26, 27, 28, 29, 30, 32, 33 (steps 2-5), 34 (bot R), 35, 36, 37 (step 1 & 5), 39, 41 (step 10 & bot R), 42, 43, 44, 46, 47, 48, 49, 50, 51, 52, 53, 54, 55, 56, 58, 60, 61, 62 (top R), 63, 64, 65, 66 (top L & mid L), 67, 68, 70, 71, 72, 73, 74, 75, 77, 78, 80 (mid), 81 (bot), 82 (bot), 83 (top & bot), 84 (mid), 87 (top & bot), 88 (mid), 89, 90, (top & mid), 91 (top & bot), 92 (top), 93 (bot), 94 (top & mid), 95 (mid & bot), 96 (bot), 97 (bot), 98 (top & bot), 99 (top), 100 (mid), 102 (mid), 103 (top & mid), 104 (mid), 105 (mid), 106, 107 (bot), 110 (mid & bot), 111, 112 (mid & bot), 113 (mid & bot), 114 (top & mid)

OTHER PHOTOGRAPHY AND ILLUSTRATION

TIM BUTLER: pgs. 88 (bot), 92 (mid), 98 (mid), 102 (bot), 107 (top), 109 (bot), 114 (bot)

KYLE CHESSER: pg. 62, (bot L)

DOUG DEALEY: pgs. 4 (bot), 34 (top L)

ROBERT J. DOLEZAL: pgs. *iv (bot)*, 5, 8 (mid L), 24 (bot L), 38, 113 (top)

REED ESTABROOK: pgs. 40, 41 (steps 5-9)

IMAGEPOINT: pgs. 14 (top R), 33 (step 1), 37 (steps 2, 3, 4, 6), 59, 92 (bot), 99 (bot)

DONNA KRISCHAN: Cover photograph and pgs. 15 (top L), 22, 66 (bot L), 76

JERRY PAVIA: pg. 80 (top & bot), 81 (top & mid), 82 (top & mid), 83 (mid), 84 (top & bot), 85, 86 (top & mid), 88 (top), 90 (bot), 93 (top), 94 (bot), 95 (top), 96 (mid), 97 (top & mid), 99 (mid), 100 (top & bot), 101 (top & mid), 102 (top), 103 (bot), 104 (top & bot), 108 (mid & bot), 109 (mid), 110 (top), 112 (top)

CHARLES SLAY: pgs. 86 (bot), 87 (mid), 93 (mid), 96 (top), 101 (bot), 105 (top & bot), 107 (mid), 108 (top), 109 (top)

YVONNE WILLIAMS: pg. 91 (mid)

ILLUSTRATIONS: HILDEBRAND DESIGN

ACKNOWLEDGEMENTS

The editors acknowledge with grateful appreciation the contribution to this book of Alden Lane Nursery, Livermore, California; and to the following individuals: Betsy Niles and Janet Tiffany.

LANDSCAPING WITH PERENNIALS

Author
Elizabeth Navas Finley

Photographer
John M. Rickard

Series Concept
Robert J. Dolezal

CREATIVE
PUBLISHING
international

Minnetonka, Minnesota

635.932
FIN

CONTENTS

INTRODUCTION

I am an earth person, one of those women who must get her fingers into soil every day.

Growing up in a California suburb where gardens were grass, ivy, and an occasional geranium, it took a trip to England to open my eyes to beautiful perennial gardens. There, in landscapes big and small, famous and anonymous, I saw how English gardeners combined these flowering plants into lush, living tapestries of color, shape, and form.

I came back to write about perennial gardening in articles for the *San Francisco Chronicle*, where I spent 17 years as a journalist, and to design gardens for my family and others. Here in the West, we favor Mediterranean herbs, sage, and iris on warm, dry hillsides, and plant lenten rose and bleeding-heart in the shade beneath redwoods. As my interest in gardening expanded, I completed the training program to become a certified Master Gardener, gaining a scientific base for my self-taught gardening.

" *To devise living pictures from simple well-known flowers seems to me the best thing to do in gardening…Whether the arrangement is simple and modest, whether it is bold and gorgeous, whether it is obvious or whether it is subtle, the aim is always to use the plants to form pictures of living beauty.* "

GERTRUDE JEKYLL
*Colour Schemes for the
Flower Garden, 1936.*

My constant teacher has been my garden. The lilies that thrived and those that sulked persuaded me to dig their holes deep and fill them with the best compost. The screaming magenta campions (they were supposed to be white!) planted among the pale alstroemerias showed how a sharp color energizes pastels.

The birds and bugs demonstrated that they could take care of garden pests if I just let them. I laid my spray bottles aside and watched as flocks of bushtits ate the aphids and the ladybug larvae scavenged where they wished. When intervention was needed—I had a plague of root weevils notching flowers and leaves—I researched low-impact approaches and finally rid my garden of the weevils by using parasitic nematodes to attack their overwintering larvae, without disturbing any of the beneficial insects.

A big thrill was learning how to make good soil by composting clippings. I use a simple "let it rot" approach filling big bins—circles of plastic fencing 5 feet (1.5 m) in diameter—with alternate layers of green material—tender green prunings, lawn trimmings, bloomed out flowers—and brown material —dried leaves and straw. When the weather is dry I hose the pile down, and when it rains, I throw a plastic tarp over it so the pile stays as moist as a wrung-out sponge. When one bin is full, I begin another. After six months, the trimmings in the first bin are reduced to dark, fragrant, fluffy compost that I shovel onto my perennials each year to make the soil more alive and the plants healthier.

For me, gardening is a continuous cycle of doing, learning, and enjoying. A perennial garden is a living picture available to everyone who wanders out into the yard with a shovel and an idea. In time, it becomes part of who we are. As gardeners, we get to grow along with our plants.

Flowering perennials are the dazzlers of the garden. Blooming in every color, size, and shape, from the blue sentinels of delphinium to the bold statement of a red-hot poker, perennials put on a show of garden color that is more lush and beautiful with each passing year. Flowering perennials mark the seasons of the year, heralding spring, summer, and autumn much as special holidays mark the calendar.

According to horticulturists, perennials are plants with fibrous roots that grow and bloom for more than two years. Annuals, on the other hand, grow, bloom, set seed, and die in one season. Perennials differ from shrubs such as rhododendrons that also grow and bloom repeatedly, because shrubs have woody stems that perennials lack.

While many perennials have long blooming seasons, growth stops in a dormant phase. Herbaceous perennials, including plantain lilies, lose their leaves in winter. Others, including Shasta daisies, keep a low tuft of foliage. In areas of mild winter climates, some flowering perennials such as lily-of-the-Nile and golden marguerite are fully evergreen.

Because perennials are permanent plants, they are practical, saving you the effort and expense of replanting your garden each year. For the most part, perennials are sturdy plants able to grow in many climates and soils, in sun and shade. Even fancy, hybridized versions are descendants of hardy wildflowers that grow in meadows, mountains, swamps, and woodlands. Since they come from many different environments, there are flowering perennials to suit nearly every garden situation.

Landscaping with perennials allows you to create attractive seasonal effects for all areas of your yard. Using the ideas presented on the following pages, you'll discover a place for perennials, whatever your garden's size or landscape's style.

Pretty and practical, flowering perennials offer a rainbow of color for any style garden

Beautiful Perennial Landscapes

Flowering perennials make every yard come alive with their colors, scents, and beautiful foliage. Perennials are the perfect complement for your landscape beds and borders, and they'll give back their gift of beauty for many years to come.

COLOR-THEMED GARDENS

Perennials can be used in a painterly way in the garden, since they bloom in a brilliant range of colors from orange daylilies to blue violet sage and yellow green hellebore to rich scarlet lobelia. Garden color design can be monochromatic, featuring a mass of one color achieved by planting flowers all within the same color range, or multihued, with complementary and contrasting shades. Choose your perennials' foliage and bloom colors to accent or coordinate with existing landscape colors such as those of your home, or in the leaf and bloom colors of trees and shrubs.

Both foliage and bloom colors allow you to set moods and play with depth perception. For example, blue-tinged hues of violet, lavender, and pink seem to recede, while warm yellows, oranges, and reds seem to advance toward you. Planting a small terrace with a garden of pink, blue, and lavender blooms makes it appear larger, while a border of gold and scarlet daylilies around a vast lawn makes the space seem cozier. Strong, contrasting colors make the most of sunny sites at midday. White is most visible as twilight comes on and is ideal for gardens enjoyed in the evening.

(Top) Red-hot poker usually is featured in perennial plantings for its distinctive, fire-red form. It also is available in brilliant yellow orange varieties. The combination of unusual form and color make it a good choice for colorful plantings.

Colors change the garden's mood, too. Generally, cool blues, lavenders, and violets are considered calming colors, while warm scarlets, oranges, and yellows are more energizing. A garden that projects a reserved and dignified tone calls for sober blue to pink tones, while a lively and gregarious front border is best with hot reds and yellows, or nearby family colors, such as coral, lemon, and pale melon.

(Right) Shades of blue and pink are natural color companions, as seen here in a seaside planting of pink stock with the sapphire spires of viper's bugloss, also known as tower of jewels.

From the first green sprouts of spring to the last wispy grasses poking through slowly accumulating snow, perennial plants provide a changing garden show and signal the turn of the seasons.

To create a garden with continuous color, organize plantings according to each plant's bloom season, which can last from weeks to months. Your challenge is to create continuous color through the wise selection of plants. When planning a succession of blooms, begin with the end of the season—from the heat of August until the first frost in October or later in warm areas—and work backwards through summer and spring. Allow time for sprouting, blooming, and entering into dormancy. Some blooms are lovely in their dried state or as they go to seed. Leave blooms with appealing seed heads to serve as food for birds and provide visual interest through autumn.

Select a highlight plant for each season or partial season: early spring, spring, early summer, summer, and autumn. Mild-climate areas may have some hardy plants in bloom throughout the winter. With a mass of blooming plants getting all the attention, the process of other plants sprouting or fading will be ignored.

Create a series of focal points at various points of your garden—such as the border near a patio or a bed near the deck. Install plants that bloom when you are most likely to use that area of your yard.

Having even a few plants in bloom each season can have considerable impact in your yard. Add a few hardy asters or perennial sunflowers to the back of the border, tuck Japanese anemones into a spot of dry shade under trees, and plant toad lilies in a bank of shady ground cover. Your garden will offer surprises throughout the growing season.

Use good gardening practices to promote healthy growth, extend the bloom season, and keep your garden tidy and enjoyable year-round [see Pruning and Promoting Continual Blooms, pgs. 70–71].

SEASONAL SUCCESSION OF BLOOMS

(Inset) An early-season display of iris, foxglove, bleeding-heart, and narcissus welcomes spring in a raised-bed planter.

(Bottom) By midyear, spring's plants have finished their display and have been replaced by lupine, dianthus, and daisy. Such successional plantings ensure a continual display of color in your landscape.

FLOWERING BORDERS AND BEDS

(Inset) A perennial border in a full-sun location requires strong primary colors to appear bright. Here, white Shasta daisies tower over golden marguerite.

(Bottom) An island bed in a shady site glows with pastel shades and features a central design that can be viewed from many angles. A blue spruce anchors the bed. Large purple coneflower and chrysanthemum mix with smaller perennial flowers at the bed's edge.

Perennial gardening at its most glamorous is represented by the classic flowering border or bed. Layered masses of blooming plants create a changing tapestry of shape and color carefully choreographed throughout the growing season. The art of the perennial border was brought to its pinnacle in the early years of the 20th century, when vast borders flanked lawns at entrances to stately homes, along with a small army of gardeners to tend them.

Many historic gardens are preserved and open to the public, through the Garden Conservancy in the United States and the National Trust in Britain. The best places to see new perennial borders are botanical gardens such as Wave Hill in New York or Van Dusen Gardens in Vancouver, British Columbia.

A border is a planting area that is long and narrow and viewed from a single side. It can be backed by hedges, fences, your home, or other structures. By comparison, a bed is a planting area that is viewed from more than one side, as an island or peninsula. Beds and borders can be formal—squares, rectangles, or circles—or informal—free-form, curving shapes. Beds can include a tree or stand alone.

Beds and borders both have their advantages. Borders leave open space in the center of the landscape and soften the edges of buildings, fences, and walkways. Beds, with two sides, can be viewed from several parts of the garden and allow sunlight and air circulation around the plants. Whichever appeals to you and fits your needs, a bed or border packed with flowers will be the glamour queen of your garden.

One big flower show from massed plantings of a single species—iris, oriental poppies, purple coneflower—is another way for you to make a colorful and dramatic perennial garden. It's an ideal approach for gardens in regions with short growing seasons or those that are viewed primarily at one time of the year.

A great example where massed perennials create dazzling shows is found in Giverny, France, at the restored home and garden of painter Claude Monet. There, you'll find spectacular plantings of bearded iris in luscious colors lining a path. For 4–8 weeks, the iris reigns supreme—and then what happens? How does the show continue after the star has retired?

Fortunately, there are available options that have worked for many gardeners. One idea is to plant early-blooming bearded irises along the edges of deep beds and behind them plant late-season bloomers such as hardy asters. That way, after blooming, the iris foliage creates a foreground for taller plants behind. Another idea is to fill beds with spring-blooming irises and between them plant summer-into-autumn-blooming perennials. Either way, choose plants that take the same sun and water conditions as iris.

For the maximum flowering period, select varieties that bloom in early season, at midseason, and also late in the season to lengthen a show of a favorite plant. Hybridizers recently have been crossing and selecting for the ability to rebloom, and now there are daylilies and other perennials that bloom repeatedly until frost threatens. With these, even gardeners devoted to a single perennial species can enjoy a long season of beautiful color in the garden.

FEATURED FLOWERS

A massed perennial planting dazzles the eye with repeated flower forms; here English daisies were planted in shades of white, red, and pink. Featuring a single species in a massed planting is a good way to create form in landscape settings where grade, slope, elevation, or planting beds exhibit little change.

MIXED PLANTINGS

Creating mixed perennial gardens is thoroughly eclectic. In a return to the spirit of the old-fashioned cottage garden, these beds and borders present perennials with your favorite shrubs, bulbs, herbs, and even food crops.

Mixed plantings can be formal or casual. Both allow you to vary color, texture, fragrance, and blooming times in your landscape. Formal plantings are arranged symmetrically. Heights are established carefully with tall plants—perhaps an evergreen shrub—in the back of the border or the center of the bed. The midsize plants are placed next, including many flowering perennials. In the foreground are smaller plants such as bulbs and annuals. Ground covers fill the space at the bed's edge.

In casual, mixed-planting styles, more attention is placed on overall ambiance, with less on height and symmetry. These quirky and colorful gardens have much to attract attention and enjoy.

Evergreen shrubs add their solid masses to the back of the border and provide creeping perennials a surface over which to scramble. Dwarf conifers lend distinctive shape to the flower border when winter falls and it's dusted with snow.

Early-flowering bulbs provide late winter color; in mixed plantings their yellowing leaves later are hidden beneath the growing perennial foliage. Summer-blooming bulbs create seasonal surprises, while fall-blooming bulbs provide welcomed garden color during the sparse late August to October season [see Combining Bulbs with Perennials, pg. 54].

Annuals with short-lived but profuse flowers fill in times of the year when your various perennials are between blooms. Many annual flowers attract the pollinating bees and hummingbirds that also serve your perennials. Whether your perennial garden is a lavish border or a single window box, it's a good idea to mix it up.

(Inset) Mixed plantings, whether in containers or in the garden, use the strength of perennial flowers against a backdrop of annual blooms or perennial shrubs.

(Bottom) Different plant heights and groupings give the border visual relief to contrast with paths, garden structures, or building materials. Such effects are best created with mixed plantings of annuals, perennials, biennials, and bulbs.

The term "natural garden" has come to mean three different things. A garden can be natural in style, natural in the selection of plants, or natural in maintenance:

Natural style: Informal and rustic gardens are designed to resemble a naturally occurring site—often a nearby meadow, prairie, desert, or marsh. Natural gardens are casual and asymmetrical; plants are set out in apparently random masses without apparent order and form. Many perennials, especially grasses, have an informal look appropriate for natural-style gardens. Structures and accents are informal, often also using materials found in the surrounding area. Natural style is ideal for more than country gardens—it fits perfectly in the city and suburbs, too.

Native plant gardening: Gardens featuring only regionally indigenous plants are beautiful, easy to maintain, require less care, and are great for attracting birds and butterflies. Some natural gardens have strict parameters of native-only plants, while others include plants that, while well adapted to the climate and soil, are native to other regions.

Environmentally friendly gardening: These natural gardens are maintained with an eye to organic remedies in preference to garden chemicals. Most perennials are sturdy and pest resistant, making them a good choice for such gardens. Environmentally friendly gardeners improve the soil and learn about natural remedies for pests and diseases in order to create a garden that is healthy for birds, bees, butterflies, children, and pets. They choose organic compost and natural fertilizers in preference to synthetic options. Any style garden can be maintained in accordance with these principles, whether it's natural in style or uses native plants.

NATURAL-STYLE GARDENS

Any landscape can adapt to a natural look, whether coastal seashore, arid region, prairie meadow, or woodland bower. Study wildlands and note their plant communities when setting out to design a natural garden.

SHADE PERENNIALS

Shade perennials transform dark, often ignored parts of the garden into woodland tapestries of leaf and flower. There are many degrees of shade, and each supports a different kind of perennial garden.

Full shade is the densest of all. Also called heavy shade, it's found under mature evergreens or along the north sides of buildings in areas of the garden that receive little sunlight throughout the year. To create a perennial garden in full shade, seek out plants that thrive in the low light and often moist conditions found under established trees and shrubs.

Dappled shade is found under deciduous trees where patterns of sun and shade move across the garden with the hour. Dappled shade is ideal for the great majority of shade plants if the soil is enriched and the area is sheltered from hot dry winds. Choose plants including bluebell, bluestar, false indigo, lilyturf, plantain lily, and trillium.

Bright shade can be found at the outer edges of tree canopies in spots that receive sun in early morning and evening hours. This is the place for perennials that take partial shade, including columbine, daylily, and foxglove.

Woodland glades, with quiet colors and fern accents, are just one style of shade garden. Create a tropical look with big-leafed perennials and the exotic blooms of daylilies; add a palm and flowering annuals in summer. An Asian-style garden takes low-key, textural perennials such as lilyturf, spring-blooming primroses, and fall-blooming toad lily.

Shade gardens are filled with perennials that thrive in dim light and flowers that delight the senses: plantain lily (top) sports blooms during summer, while wake robin (center) signals the arrival of spring.

(Bottom) Hydrangea require moist, acidic soil rich in organic matter to achieve their intense blue and purple colors. If the color of your shade plants begins to dim, a feeding with acidic fertilizer may be due.

PERENNIALS IN CONTAINERS

Sturdy and adaptable perennials grow well in containers and make good companions to flowering annuals and bulbs.

There are many reasons to grow perennials in containers: It's easy—you avoid digging and soil tests—just pour ideal soil out of a bag. Containers also let you create a show of color in difficult to plant places—decks and patios, of course, and also garden areas where the soil is filled with roots or other obstructions. In cold climates you can grow tender perennials and simply move them indoors when frigid weather hits. Best of all, container plantings allow you to experiment with new arrangements, textures and color combinations.

When creating container gardens, big pots are better than small. Mimic a lavish border or bouquet by selecting plants in these four categories:

Anchor: This is an upright plant, 2–3 feet (60–90 cm) high, for the center or back of the pot. Long-blooming plants, including golden marguerite and fleabane , are good subjects.

Infill: These are long-blooming plants, 6–18 inches (15–45 cm) high, to surround the base of the anchor, which often is spindly. Plants with interesting foliage make wonderful infill plants, and plants such as plantain lilies and silvery- or maroon-leafed coralbells guarantee a long season of color.

Fluffer: These are supporting players with small-scale leaves and flowers, including thrift, spurge, and stonecrops. Plant dense, fluffy specimens along the rim of the pot to hide bare soil and stems and complete the lush, abundant look of the container.

Draper: These plants spill over the pot's edge. Some drapers, including wild strawberry, are bushy enough to replace fluffers, and a flowering draper can take over the functions of infill and fluffer plants under an anchor.

Design a window box with fewer categories of plants. Place an infill plant such as pincushion flower or small sage at the back of the box and two or more fluffers and drapers to cover the front.

When shopping for container plants, hold one potted plant next to another to check the effect. The process is similar to the way you hold a tie or scarf against a shirt and suit when accessorizing your clothes to find combinations that please and excite you.

(Top left) Hanging containers filled with fuschia have long been popular plantings beneath shade structures. They require daily watering and protection from direct sunlight during the hottest hours of the day.

(Bottom) Tender geraniums are grown as perennials in mild-winter climates. They require shelter in cold-winter climates. Plant them in containers and move them indoors as temperatures cool and they become dormant, but before first frosts are expected.

After viewing the array of beautiful gardens on the last few pages, you'll be inspired to create a perennial garden of your own. This chapter takes you through the decision-making process so you can make informed choices concerning landscape design, plant selection, and garden projects. You'll find help in determining the location, purpose, size, and scope of your garden. Included is a guide to the skills, materials, tools, and equipment you'll need to install and maintain your new landscape. Of course, selecting plants is a high priority for a garden, and there are ideas here on how to find plants that are right for you. Finally, if you're new to gardening, there are suggestions on the sources and resources available to learn more about perennial gardens.

Bring the colorful world of perennial plants into your garden with a series of simple choices

A Garden Checklist

The most important influence on gardening activities is your climate. To help you choose plants that grow well in your area, the United States Department of Agriculture [USDA] has divided the world into a series of plant hardiness zones based on the average of winter low temperatures [see USDA Plant Hardiness Around the World, pg. 115]. As you research perennial plants and begin to narrow your choices, remember that plants grow best in certain conditions. Plants are categorized by their plant hardiness zone on seed packets, by their nursery growers, and in the listings in this book [see Encyclopedia of Flowering Perennials, pg. 79].

Once you find your hardiness zone, refine that information by looking at your local topography. The lay of the land and your site's sun, shade, and wind exposure can affect your garden, making it either warmer or cooler than the surrounding area and creating a microclimate different than your neighbors'. Choosing plants that are well-adapted to your zone and your microclimate will ensure their success in your garden and ease your long-term maintenance tasks.

Purple coneflowers and foxglove form a sea of beautiful blossoms in a cottage garden setting. When the purpose of your garden is to create a buffer between your home and the street, plant irregular groups to expand the space and frame your dwelling.

UNDERSTANDING THE SITE

Whether you already have determined the site for your perennial garden or are still considering its location, it's important for you to walk around your yard and evaluate its potential for growing perennials. Most of these plants are easy to grow, but have specific needs for sun or shade, well-drained soil, and wind protection. By getting to know your site's exposure, microclimates, and soil conditions, you'll be able to select plants that will thrive in your garden.

Your microclimate, the little piece of climate found in your garden, is a huge factor in the success of individual plants. The topography of your site and even the position of your house on the lot affects the garden's microclimate. A site on the top or side of a hill is windier but less frosty than a garden in a valley. A north-facing garden is colder than a protected south-facing one. Find north on your property and mark the direction on the ground with stakes or a line of flour.

Full-sun perennials need sun six hours a day; site them in south- or west-facing locations. Part-sun perennials need four hours of morning or late afternoon sun, and do well in east- or west-facing gardens. Shade perennials prefer north-facing sites with protection from the midday sun. In moist, cool climates such as those found in the Pacific northwest and British Columbia, partial-sun perennials take more sun, while in the hot, dry southwest, they'll want more shade.

Shelter from the wind is important. A hedge, fence, or building provides a windbreak or, in an exposed area, a simple screen of lattice panels can moderate gales.

Most perennials require well-drained soil. Far more young plants die of fungal disease caused by wet soil than drought. If your soil drains poorly or is marshy, consider building a raised bed [see Raised Beds, pg. 38] or creating a marsh garden by excavating a depression for a pond and planting its edges with aquatics, including plantain lily and masterwort, that tolerate continuously damp soil.

A child's playhouse becomes a picturesque landmark when you surround it with flowering perennial borders. It's a great project to launch young gardeners within your family on a lifelong hobby. Be sure to share with them the garden's care, too. Give them the gift of their very own gardening tools.

In addition to providing color and beauty, perennial gardens can serve a purpose in your yard. As permanent plants, perennials accent or hide other elements on the site, attract or repel wildlife, and increase your enjoyment of the space. As you choose sites for perennial plants, consider their use. Your garden's special purpose helps you decide questions of location, size, building materials, and type of plants.

Some uses call out for specific plants. For a kitchen garden, think how a lovely surrounding hedge of lavender and accents of sage will expand your culinary pleasure while it hides the functional areas of your yard. If you love to spend evenings relaxing on your patio, place nearby white and pale yellow flowers that open at twilight such as evening primrose and night-blooming daylily.

To expand your children's interest in gardening, locate perennials near a playhouse and delight their senses with fragrant plants such as sweet violet and lots of flowers to pick: Shasta daisy, false indigo, and tickseed. Avoid hazardous plants such as foxglove and monkshood; their foliage, stems, and roots contain toxic compounds.

For a garden habitat that attracts birds and butterflies, choose a sunny spot sheltered from wind, provide a ready source of water, and avoid using garden chemicals. Lure these beautiful creatures with their favorite foods. Adult butterflies sip nectar from the tiny flowers of most daisylike flowers, while their larvae chew on foliage. Seed-eating birds will snack on purple coneflowers, among others, while hummingbirds will whir and flicker around sages, lupines, and red-hot pokers.

PURPOSE AND PERENNIAL GARDENS

(Left) Screen seldom-used areas of your yard with perennials. Paths in such areas can be more decorative than functional.

(Right, below) Hide pool equipment, air conditioner condensers, sheds, and other yard equipment behind a wall planted with perennial vines. Here, morning glory does the job. Another choice would be trumpet vine.

(Bottom) Define your outdoor rooms with a decorative edging that also attracts colorful visitors. Wild birds and butterflies find the seeds and flowers of many perennial plants a favored food source. Choose plants that have deep throats that bear nectar if your goal is to entice hummingbirds and butterflies, those that develop seed heads to attract other bird species.

SCALING THE PROJECT

A perennial garden can be as small as a window box or extend for 100 feet (30 m) as a meadow or border. The determining factors are how much space is available and your available time for garden care. Consider starting small, perhaps planting only one section each year and covering the rest in a weed-smothering mulch. Scale your garden according to your time and space. There are plenty of perennials for people with limited time.

Maintenance time depends on the garden's size, the number of different plants it contains, and the overall level of neatness you prefer. The garden style has an impact on maintenance as well. In a formal garden, the perennials must be kept as tidy as the clipped hedges that frame them, whereas the same plants in a casual meadow look delightfully natural as they go to seed [see Caring for Flowering Perennials, pg. 57].

Reduce maintenance time in the perennial garden by choosing plants that suit your conditions and grow well in your climate. Using fewer varieties of plants and selecting plants that look good throughout the garden season results in less planting time. Container plantings may be small yet can be high maintenance, since they require daily watering in hot weather. Installing drip irrigation on automatic timers is a popular, time-saving remedy.

Large acreage, especially that of hillside yards with changing elevations, is best served by clearly defined beds and borders. Use trees as a perimeter back-drop, then terrace the slopes with low walls and sweeping plantings.

For example, a low-upkeep perennial planting in partial shade might include leafy bellflower, early-blooming lenten rose, late-spring foxglove, and August-blooming anemone. Once established, these easygoing plants will provide color changes and continuity with just 30 minutes of grooming performed every two weeks. Enjoy their cool, green foliage during the summer's heat. If you want to add more plants for color and texture, place them in the most visible parts of your landscape: adjacent to the house or next to paths, steps, benches, and gates.

Focus attention in small-space gardens by using every surface: ground, wall, and overhead. Remember that perennials are natural companions to window-box containers. Perch them on shelves beneath windows and along the tops of garden walls where they will be seen both from indoor locations and will be at eye level outdoors.

Although the final shape and planting arrangement of your perennial garden is determined by your design [see Decorating with Flowering Perennials, pg. 23], the width from front to back is based on practical needs. The minimum width of a bed or border is 3 feet (90 cm), allowing for two layers of plants. The maximum width of the bed depends on your reach when tending it, usually about 3½ feet (1.1 m). Because a peninsula or island bed can be tended from both sides, it can be as wide as 7 feet (2.1 m), while a border that size needs rear access.

A good ratio of the flower border to the overall land-scape space is 1:2. For example, in a space 30 feet (9 m) wide, the lawn or patio would take up two-thirds of the space or 20 feet (6 m), and the perennials one-third or 10 feet (3 m), perhaps as two beds 5 feet (1.5 m) wide.

It's best to consider adding structural features to your perennial garden—a raised bed, gazebo, arbor, path, walls or accents of natural stones, even a small pond—well before you pick your plants. Choose finishes that coordinate with your garden style: crisp bricks or pavers for a formal garden path or meandering stepping stones for an informal garden. Look for balance between the overall garden space and the size of the feature.

GARDEN FORM AND ELEMENTS

(Left) Plan defining elements of your landscape prior to planting. Here, low-voltage lighting was installed to enhance safety after dark and extend the hours of garden enjoyment.

(Below) Keep architectural improvements in scale and match their design to the garden style you have selected. The orderly structure of this picket fence's repeating elements is a good match for the profusion of flowers planted nearby in a perennial border.

SKILLS AND MATERIALS

As you determine your garden's needs, also assess your own. Do you have the ability to install and maintain this garden yourself? Do you have the desire and resources to have others do some or all of the work for you? In addition to the decorative features, also consider practical systems for irrigating and lighting your yard. Both will extend the enjoyment of your garden—irrigation by lessening the effort of maintenance and lighting by extending its hours of use. Will you need to add an irrigation system to your garden? Will it be a high-pressure spray system or a low-pressure drip? Will you add path and plant lighting? Irrigation systems and low-voltage lighting are good do-it-yourself projects, although a few hours of professional help may be needed. For example, consider a tradesperson to pull an electrical line out into the garden if none exists, or tap into the water supply line and install the valves, backflow preventors, and controller. Afterwards you can install low-voltage wiring and fixtures or lay the irrigation lines to the plants.

If you have an established yard, consider the elements—both growing and built—already in place and decide if you want to keep or lose them in your new design. Are there trees or shrubs that need pruning to let in more light? Overgrown shrubs can be reduced or pruned into small, graceful trees. Will your perennial garden replace lawn? If so, the turfgrass must be completely removed to avoid resprouting [see Preparing the Site, pg. 32].

Look at existing paths, patios, and garden walls and assess how to incorporate them into your perennial garden or the methods required for removal. As you review the tasks in your project, take an inventory of your skills. Are you comfortable with carpentry, plumbing, pruning, general tinkering, and fixing? Consider your tolerance for tasks such as hauling heavy loads of soil or stones? Do you have knowledgeable friends or relatives who will help? Above all, be realistic about your time, energy, and abilities.

Creating an edging of bricks set in sand to frame a bed is an easy choice for defining a planting area and makes its care easier. Other options include bricks set in mortar, masonry construction, and a poured-concrete edging—each require more time and effort than this simple solution.

TOOLS AND EQUIPMENT

Y ou need quality tools to do a proper job of installing and maintaining your garden. Before beginning any of the building or planting projects in this book, read the instructions for each one to make sure you have the right equipment. Check your storage area for the following implements and materials, and prepare a list of needed items that must be acquired.

For digging and soil preparation choose a sturdy shovel or spade. A wide-bladed variety, 1 foot (30 cm) across, is useful for moving soil or mulch, while a small, 6-inch (15-cm) border spade is ideal for digging into an already planted bed. For trenching, consider also a narrow, square, deep-bladed trenching shovel.

You will do a lot of clipping to keep your garden tidy, so choose the best, most comfortable hand pruner you can afford. Select models with bypass blades that cut cleanly, rather than anvil blades that crush plant stems. You also may need long-handled loppers to cut branches over ½ inch (13 mm) in diameter and hedge shears for quick pruning jobs. Add a folding pruning saw for thick stems and woody branches.

For weeding and cultivating, acquire a hand trowel, dandelion weeder, and a narrow hand rake. Put them in a convenient tool caddie along with a kneeling cushion and comfortable, well-fitting gloves. Among the best gloves are inexpensive cotton knits dipped in latex, although some people prefer leather gloves.

Keep an array of fertilizers on hand including organics and synthetic granules, encapsulated synthetics for container plantings, solid organics for soil improvement, spikes, tablets, and liquid versions for spraying using a hose-end sprayer or application with a watering can.

Create a potting area in your garden with general-purpose tools, including a bucket, tarp, and wheelbarrow; a table; bags of mulch and potting soil; stakes; ties; labels; and a composter to turn garden clippings into rich compost.

Establish your own personal weather station with a rain gauge and a minimum/maximum thermometer—this is one that records the lowest and highest temperature for a period of time and is reset with a magnet. Add a notebook to record temperatures, precipitation, and garden observations and you're on your way to becoming an expert on your land.

Your garden will need a variety of materials: dry and liquid fertilizers, mulch, compost, and both pressure hand and hose-end sprayers. Supplies are readily available at garden centers, nurseries, hardware stores, and mass merchants.

TOOLS

Hoe
Spade
Gloves
Lopping shears
Watering can
Pail
Trug
Hand fork and trowels
Pruning saw
Hand pruning shears
Spray bottle
Garden clogs

PLANTING CHOICES

Narrow your planting choices by first seeking out plants that grow best in your area. Visit local plant nurseries and garden centers, especially those with display gardens.

While looking at the various plants, also investigate the places they are offered. Choose plants from establishments with a good selection of the variety of plants you want for your garden. Best are retailers where everything is well marked, the stock is replenished regularly, and the plants are healthy and well tended. Nursery and garden center personnel can be a great resource as you make garden design and plant selection decisions. Check that garden expertise is available to answer your questions both before and after the plants are placed in your garden.

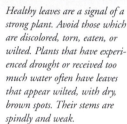

Healthy leaves are a signal of a strong plant. Avoid those which are discolored, torn, eaten, or wilted. Plants that have experienced drought or received too much water often have leaves that appear wilted, with dry, brown spots. Their stems are spindly and weak.

Many perennials are sold in a variety of forms. Now is the time to determine the one that is best for you. Perennials are available for purchase as seed, in several different sizes of small, so-called six-pack nursery containers, and in pots ranging from 2 inches (50 mm) to 5 gallons (19 l).

As you choose and later arrange your plants, check for each of the following: Are there contrasts in foliage color, leaf size, and shape? Is there variety in plant sizes and shapes? Are there contrasts in color, shapes, and sizes of blooms? Does the plant arrangement fit your chosen garden theme? When you research and visit retailers, create a perennial wish list that is custom-designed for your garden's climate, exposure, and special purpose. Start by gathering all your plant information sources: the plant encyclopedia in the back of this book, periodicals, plant catalogs, information from local garden experts, and sources in the electronic marketplace.

Choose your garden center or nursery from those that have a broad selection of fresh plants and a knowledgeable staff. Stores with heavy traffic often have the best choice of plants and an inventory of frequently replenished stock.

Set up a perennial wish list on paper or use computer spreadsheet software. Across its top, list plant choice categories that are important to you. Include your desires: seasonal color, featured flowers, growing natives, attracting butterflies; your garden's purpose: blocking wind, providing cut flowers, establishing a border; and your site conditions: sun, shade, soil condition, exposure. Also list bloom color, bloom season, and mature plant height. Allow as much space as possible for notes or special conditions about individual plants.

As you discover plants of interest, list their common and scientific names in a column down the left side of the page. Fill in as much information as possible about the plants you expect to enjoy in your garden.

There's a huge amount of wisdom on gardening, as anyone who has browsed a garden center bookshelf, viewed cable TV, or skimmed data electronically can testify. To organize this information, collect favorite photos, finish material samples, information sources, and notes in a design idea file. You'll find this file and your perennial wish list valuable tools as you begin to develop your garden plan [see Designing a Formal Perennial Border, Planning Plant Arrangements, and Designing a Casual Perennial Bed, pgs. 27–29].

SOURCES AND RESOURCES

Especially if you are new to your area, learn as much as possible about the climate and plants that do well locally. Make your first stop a public library for information collected by your town on its weather and climate. Check the shelves for gardening books by local authors. Look in the governmental pages of your local phone book for the USDA county cooperative or Agriculture Canada extension office; both are a gold mine of information on local growing conditions. Many extensions have a Master Gardener program, with trained volunteers who answer questions from home gardeners and help to identify plants as well as pests and diseases.

(Top) Catalogs and periodicals are a fresh source each season of new perennial varieties. Use them as an information resource.

(Bottom) Electronic sources of information are readily available via computer and telephone. Many direct merchants and publishers now provide detailed gardening information. Remember to check the data you receive from such sources for accuracy, both for your garden's plant hardiness zone and for its climate conditions.

Do outdoor research by walking in your neighborhood to gain design inspiration as well as plant ideas. See what grows well, particularly visiting older neighborhoods to see which plants are thriving over time. Check out public botanical gardens, historic homes with restored grounds, and private residences open for garden tours. Look for gardens designed in your chosen style or that serve a purpose similar to the one you hope to achieve. Seek out local garden clubs. Clubs often welcome non-members and new gardeners to their social and educational events at public sites or in special private gardens. Garden clubs will provide you knowledge, inspiration, and advice from people who are enthusiastic about gardening in your area. Everywhere you go, ask questions: What's that plant? Does it grow well here? Where can I get it? Generally, gardeners everywhere love talking about their plants.

Search electronically for plant societies, growers, gardens to visit, and electronic retailers. Visit the site of the Perennial Plant Association, a group of growers who award the Perennial Plant of the Year [see On-line, pg. 118].

PERENNIAL PLANNING FLOWCHART

A flowchart is a planning tool that allows you to scan the important questions that need to be answered as you plan your garden. In landscaping as in most other projects, there is a sequence in which tasks should be done. By planning an orderly flow of tasks and arranging for tools and materials to be on site when needed, you can reduce wasted time and duplicated effort. As you go through the following questions you can also develop the timetable for your project.

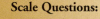

1 Site Choice Questions:
What zone does your garden match on the USDA plant hardiness zone map? How long is your frost-free growing season? Do the natural features of your site create a microclimate that is warmer or cooler than the surrounding region? Will your perennial garden face North, South, East, or West? Is it windy? From what directions do summer and winter winds come? Does your site have poorly drained soil? Will your new garden affect your neighbor's landscape? What must you do to improve conditions to grow the plants you want?

UNDERSTANDING YOUR SITE

DETERMINING GOALS

2 Goal Questions:
What is the purpose of this garden: To accent a garden feature? Hide a view? Offer special plants? Teach children about nature? Attract wild creatures? Be part of a garden for food crops? How much time do you have to install and care for a perennial garden? Have you established a design idea file? Have you chosen a landscape design style that complements your home and region? What are your resources, skills, and budget? Which items are indispensable now and which can be added in later phases?

CHOOSING SITE IMPROVEMENTS

3 Scale Questions:
How much space do you have for a perennial garden? Have you designed your proposed garden to see if it is the right scale and shape for the rest of your yard? Are there structural features associated with your perennial garden? Will you install gazebos, arbors, ponds, paths, or raised beds? Will you add decorative accessories? Where will you locate a bench, birdbath, or sundial? Will you install an irrigation system or retrofit an existing one? Spray or drip? Will you install low-voltage lighting for nighttime viewing?

4 **Plant Selection Questions:**
Is a soil test needed? Will you use a home test kit or send a sample to a laboratory? Have you completed your perennial wish list? Will the plants you desire thrive in your soil? Do you need to amend the soil? Are the plants you want well adapted to your climate? Have you selected plants with compatible blooming times to provide season-long color? Have you located garden retailers in your area with a good inventory of perennials? How many plants and what sizes will you need? Do you know the preferred propagation method for your plants? Have you determined a planting schedule that will suit each plant and propagation form? Are you available at these planting times and can you provide follow-up care until the plants are established?

PREPARING TO PURCHASE PLANTS

ORGANIZING TIME, TOOLS, AND TASKS

5 **Preparation Questions:**
Do you have plants or other structures to be removed? Do trees or shrubs require pruning or removal? Does turf need to be removed? Will you be changing soil levels in your garden? When will the paths, walls, decks, ponds, or other structures be built? When will you install a new irrigation system or retrofit an existing one? When does a power line need to be installed? When will you establish the planting beds? How much special soil amendment do you need? How much mulch is needed? Will you choose bags or bulk? Will you bring it home or arrange delivery? Have you checked your tool storage and made a list of tools and supplies needed? How long will each task take?

FINDING HELP AND INFORMATION

6 **Resources and Aid Questions:**
What steps will you do yourself? Will you hire others to help? Where can you get information on your local climate conditions and planting dates? Where will you go to obtain information, materials, and assistance with your building projects? Are there specialists or retailers that offer classes or advice on installing irrigation and lighting systems? What are your community resources on local gardening information: neighbors? extension offices? media? garden center staff? Do any local botanical gardens, arboretums, adult education programs, nurseries, or community colleges offer gardening classes?

Transforming your perennial wish list and design idea file into an actual garden requires a garden plan. This chapter takes you through each step in the design process, with information on combining colors, developing a garden theme, and arranging plants.

A successful design—whether Monet's Giverny garden or a single bed or border—is based on what works at that specific site. As you plan the size and shape of your perennial garden, imagine how the planted bed or border will appear alongside your home. Different house architectural styles and colors suggest different approaches for structural features, bed and border shapes and sizes, and plant shapes and colors.

Look at the existing patterns in your yard: Are paths straight and do they meet at right angles? This suggests a formal design of rectangular or circular borders. If paths and lawns are casual and curving, informal curves and asymmetrical arrangements will harmonize better. If you like the lines of your garden, design your perennial bed or border to match them.

To visualize the size and shape of various elements, do a mock-up in the yard. Use a hose or flour to outline each structural feature as well as paths and bed or border sizes. Add corrugated cartons to represent mounding plants, open umbrellas for fountain shapes, stakes for spires and wands, and crumpled newspapers for horizontal plants. Check your design from all angles—especially from indoors—and modify it until you're satisfied.

Once you have a good general sense of what you want, transfer the ideas to a garden plan for fine-tuning. A garden plan is a scaled drawing for use during shopping and installation. It can be created with pencil on paper or by using a computer software program developed for the purpose.

Good garden design principles coordinate structural features and plants in pleasing combinations

Decorating with Flowering Perennials

The beauty of a gazebo is enhanced by hanging containers filled with perennial plants. It also is surrounded with lush beds of blooming plants. Such structures are available as ready-to-assemble kits or can be built from scratch.

PERENNIALS AND COLOR

Since perennials inspire colorful gardens, a little information on the subject of color helps ensure you'll have pleasing combinations.

An individual color is called a hue, and hues are arranged in groups: the primaries are red, yellow, and blue; their complements are green, violet, and orange. Between these are the intermediary hues such as yellow green. Hues may be lightened with tints or darkened with tones. Color schemes are described as

Monochromatic: Uses a single hue for all blooms such as a yellow garden. These gardens feature foliage contrasts, size variations, and shapes to create excitement.

Analogous: Includes a group of hues set next to each other on the color wheel, such as all the hues between red orange and yellow green. These groupings always look good together, but sometimes lack drama.

Complementary: Features colors opposite on the color wheel, perhaps yellow orange and blue violet. Complementary color schemes are exciting, but can be busy and distracting.

Green leaves dominate in every garden and have an effect on adjacent flower colors: reds dazzle, yellows deepen, and blues shift toward violet. Yellow green leaves brighten hot colors and contrast with blues and violets; red foliage enriches warm shades; and blue gray foliage blends with whites and pastels and cools down oranges.

White is a strong presence in the garden. White dilutes dark, rich colors; dulls yellow; brightens pastels; and sharpens red, blue, and green.

The intensity of light affects colors, too. Brilliant sunshine makes dark colors shine. Pastels glow in the shade.

The proportions of a color affect how it's perceived. For example, scarlet oriental poppies look brighter than a red-blooming Texas sage because the poppies are bigger and bolder than are the sage's diminutive flowers. If you want a bright red effect, the poppies are the right choice. If you prefer a subtle touch of red that will mix with or brighten other colors, the red sage is a better option.

A garden designer rarely works with isolated colors. They often match architectural elements when determining color choices. Check around your home and garden for color: Is paving blue, gray, tan, or red? Must plantings coordinate with walls, picket fences, or a house paint color? Use a color wheel to help establish a color palette for your garden [see Using a Color Wheel, opposite].

SEASONAL COLOR

It's sometimes a challenge to plant a garden that's colorful throughout the growing season, since weather variations from year to year can hasten or delay blooming times. The traditional approach is to devote parts of a yard to different seasons and plant accordingly, letting areas of the garden sprout, bloom, and become dormant in their off seasons. Another approach is to plant long-season flowering perennials throughout the garden, supplemented with seasonal accents from annuals, bulbs, and flowering shrubs at the times of year when the flowering perennial garden is less showy.

This captivating boat that has outlived its usefulness as a watercraft doubles as a planter for colorful perennials and bulbs. A bright red coat of paint and plants to its gunwales complete the maritime motif.

USING A COLOR WHEEL

Artists and graphic designers use a color wheel to determine combinations. Flower garden designers also benefit by planning with color in mind. Look for an artist's color wheel at art or craft retailers. Most wheels are a flat disk printed with 12 hues of varying intensities topped by a revolving disk with windows to show relationships between hues. The wheel presents the primary colors—red, yellow, and blue—across from their complements—orange, green, and violet. It also is divided between so-called warm and cool colors. To use a color wheel when you choose plants and building materials for your design, follow these easy steps:

1 Establish your first selection among the primary colors of red, yellow, and blue, matching that color to the wheel. Here, the crimson of million bells 'cherry pink' were chosen to provide a low, foundation planting.

2 Next, pick a plant complementary in color to the red—violet or purple. Here, verbena 'homestead purple' was chosen to trail down a drystack stone wall.

3 Then, find an analagous color to red—such as orange and violet. Bush lantana 'yellow gold' fills the bill for an orange, upright plant that will blend well with red.

4 In the finished bed, the red, orange, and violet plants, along with purple fountain grass and outback daisy, make a pleasing color combination.

CHOOSING A THEME

Before drawing plans for your perennial garden, review your idea file and decide on a single theme or look [see Beautiful Perennial Landscapes, pg. 1]. It might reflect your home's architecture, be an extension of the natural landscape in your locale, mirror the garden's purpose, or celebrate a favorite color or special plant.

Match the formality of your theme as you consider structural elements, determine finishes, choose garden accessories, and make planting arrangements. Formality involves symmetry and matched placement. Trees and shrubs may be pruned into columns. Plants are organized in tiers, from short ones at the edge to tall ones in back; backgrounds and front edges are crisply defined and full. An example of formal placement is when the border plantings to the left of a path mirror those on the right.

Casual planting design takes its cues from the natural world, where plants grow in irregular, asymmetrical masses that balance without matching. Plants retain their natural shapes. Tall accents are clustered to lead the eye through the planting, while bulb and annual accents are dotted about as if self-sown. Edges often are irregular, with plants growing into a gravel path or trailing over the garden's walls.

(Right) Formal gardens use straight-edged beds and carefully tended paths to define regular geometric shapes. Plants are arranged symmetically in groups and balanced to a central point.

(Bottom) Casual gardens take their theme from nature, with irregular edges, intermingled plantings, and curving pathways. Plants are grouped in odd-numbered patterns.

DESIGNING A FORMAL PERENNIAL BORDER

Formal themes require symmetry and exact plant placement. A drawing will speed the actual planting. Place plants at regular intervals and step down heights from back to front. Mirror plans to match borders; design formal beds as back-to-back borders. Gather together measurements of your site, your perennial wish list, scaled graph paper, tracing paper, pencils or markers, ruler, and tape, and follow these easy steps:

1 On graph paper, outline the site. Mark utility supply and drain lines. Show North, sun, and prevailing wind directions. Using black pencil, indicate existing structural features and plants to retain. This is your base plan.

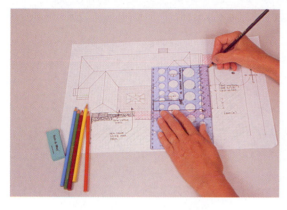

2 Attach a tracing paper overlay. Using colored pencils, draw all new structural features, paths, walls, and systems additions such as lighting or irrigation.

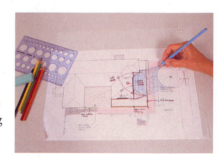

3 Add a second overlay. Space planting points at regular intervals. Working from your plant list, place tall plants at the back of the border. Add horizontal plants at the front edge and medium-height plants in between. Match plant shapes, foliage texture and shape, and bloom colors.

4 Draw a circle to scale around each planting point, indicating the plant's spread at full growth. Using pencils matched to bloom color, fill in the circles. Create pleasing color combinations and absolute symmetry.

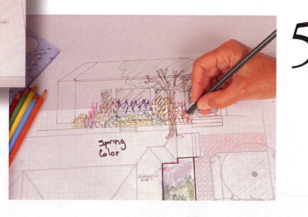

5 To visualize the bed, create an elevation—a ground-level view. Sketch the site, placing foreground plants first, followed in succession by each background plant. Use colored pencils to indicate the bloom color and plants shape.

PLANNING PLANT ARRANGEMENTS

Arranging the plants in a bed or border involves visualizing each individual plant's size and shape, its foliage appearance and texture, and its bloom color, then combining the individual plants to fit your garden theme.

Plants have distinctive shapes: mounds such low-growing thrift, medium-high lavender, and shoulder-high aster; spires including foxglove; thinner wands such as bugbane and speedwell; fountain-shaped plants including daylilies; and spreading horizontal plants such as bergenia. Two classic combinations are mounds with spires and fountains with horizontals.

When considering design factors, remember that foliage lasts longer in the garden than blooms. Leaves can be as tiny as candytuft or as big as those of Solomon's-seal. Shapes span the gamut from swordlike bearded iris to grassy lilyturf to red paddles of bergenia, from heart-shaped plantain lily to lacy bleeding-heart, from feathery yarrow to needlelike lavender.

(Right) Plants are arranged in beds according to their height. Place small plants at the edge of the bed or border, then step higher with each succeeding row towards the center or back.

(Bottom) Use fountains, bird-baths, viewing balls, or other structural elements as focal points for island beds and small borders. In larger settings, use trees and large shrubs as a central element or frame.

Leaves that are big and bold-shaped stand out, while delicate foliage blends in. The best-designed beds and borders have a variety of foliage shapes: bold-leafed bergenia, mid-sized navelwort leaves, and small, fernlike false spirea.

In formal designs, plants are arranged in drifts—long, thin groupings of three or more plants set mostly parallel to the front edge. This pattern allows the plants to blend into a tapestry of form and color. Place tall plants at the back of the border—or in the center of a bed—with low-growing plants along the edges and medium-sized ones sandwiched between. Vary the tiers occasionally to avoid rigidity.

Formal arrangements gain strength from repetition: rather than choosing different species for fall bloom, for example, choose one, perhaps a large-statured obedience plant, and repeat groups of it along the back of the border or in the center of a bed. Choose secondary plants to contrast or harmonize with the featured plant. Place the season's featured plants close enough together to make a unified group, and then distribute the secondary plants throughout the remaining space.

Casual gardens contain fewer plant species, grouped in lavish masses. For example, a vertical accent, perhaps a tall daylily, is dotted in repeated irregular clumps throughout the site, while lower-growing Shasta daisies and tickseed create masses around them. A tall, see-through plant such as purple coneflower or blanket flower might be set at the front edge, partly masking the plants and features behind and creating a frame.

Such planting arrangements allow views into the center of the garden and are ideal for deep or square sites, as long as you include a path or stepping stones to provide easy access for care of the garden.

DESIGNING A CASUAL PERENNIAL BED

Casual planting arrangements are flexible, but still have underlying organization and benefit from a garden plan. Beds differ from borders in that both sides are viewed. For a casual theme, position plants at irregular intervals, group odd numbers of plants, and vary heights from center to front. Spread plant groupings throughout the space, avoiding mirrored sides. Round off straight edges and sharp corners. Gather together measurements of the site, your perennial wish list, scaled graph paper, tracing paper, pencils or markers, ruler, and tape, and follow these easy steps:

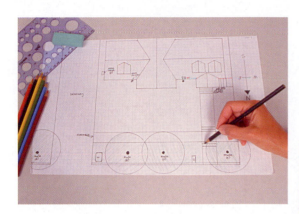

1 On graph paper, outline the planting area. Mark the location of water and electric supply lines. Show North, sun, and prevailing wind directions. Using black pencil, indicate existing structural features and plants to retain. This is your base plan.

2 Attach a tracing paper overlay. Using colored pencils, indicate new structural features, paths, walls, and system additions such as lighting or irrigation. If your design is complicated, create a color-coded key for each type of element.

3 Add a second overlay. Mark each tall plant's center point, creating groups with odd numbers and avoiding regular spacing. Place medium-height plants next, then fill remaining spaces with horizontal plants. Vary plant form, foliage shape and texture, and bloom colors.

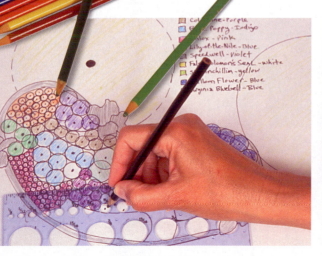

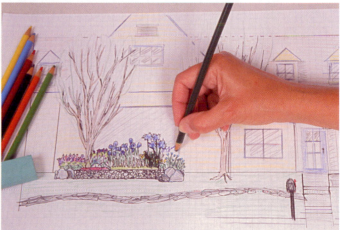

4 Draw a circle to scale around each planting point, indicating the plant's spread at full growth. Using pencils matched to bloom color, fill in the circles. Check mirrored images, color combinations, or accidental symmetry and make necessary adjustments.

5 On a separate sheet, draw a profile of the various plant heights. Confirm that groups avoid symmetrical placement and can be viewed from all sides. Count the number of each type of plant. Note the total for each species on your plant shopping list.

B efore selecting plants and putting them into the ground, make sure that the soil is ready for planting, install any new utility systems, and construct new structural features. This chapter details the process of evaluating your site, testing your soil, and improving it prior to planting. It also presents an overview of site improvements for drainage, lighting, and irrigation, and includes several step-by-step building projects to enhance your garden.

As you will discover in the plant encyclopedia, every plant has specific soil needs [see Encyclopedia of Flowering Perennials, pg. 79]. They include soil texture, drainage requirements, and acid–alkaline balance. Although testing and improving your soil requires effort, generally you need do it only once. The reward for this preparation is healthy soil, vigorous plants that grow lustily, and conditions that help plants stand up to pests and diseases.

Good garden soil is a blend of mineral particles, organic matter, air, and water. Generally, mineral particles are either sand, silt, or clay. A mixture of all three is called "loam." Organic matter is decayed vegetable and animal material.

Sandy soil mostly has large particles with space between them through which water rushes. Such soils provide ample air pockets, but drain moisture too quickly and frequently lack water-soluble nutrients. Clay soil has smaller particles, with tiny spaces that are slower to drain. Clay soils are poorly drained, may retain salts, and are deficient in oxygen.

Typical garden soil is about 45 percent mineral particles, 5 percent organic matter, 25 percent air, and 25 percent water. Soil that is less than ideal can be amended with sand, clay, and organic matter to improve it for your perennials.

> **Blooming perennials thrive in well-prepared soil with utility systems and structures in place**

Preparing to Plant Perennials

The final steps before planting your perennial plants include testing, amending, and preparing soil; making site improvements; building beds; and preparing edgings. Only after your bed or border is complete should you install your flowering plants.

PREPARING THE SITE

To assess your site's ability to grow perennials, begin by taking a good look at plants now growing there. If possible, note bloom times over the course of a garden season. In an established landscape, dormant perennial plants or bulbs may be hidden underground. If your site grows good weeds or other plants, it'll grow good perennials.

Next, clear the planting area [see Preparing and Amending Soil, pg. 35]. Ideally, prepare soil 18 inches (45 cm) deep. If your home is newly built, its soil may have been compacted during construction. Dig into the soil to remove obstructions such as tree roots or stumps, construction debris, and stone. Lawns of bluegrass and fescue can be cut below ground, and rolled up for removal. Rhizomatous grasses, including Bermuda and zoysia, must be killed before removal. One removal method is to use solarization—cover the lawn with clear plastic for 4–6 weeks at the height of summer—then use a turfing tool or sod cutting machine to remove the grass and every bit of stem and root. A faster and more certain approach for any kind of lawn is to use a systemic herbicide to kill the grass before removal, weighing carefully the impact on the environment and personal safety against convenience.

Once the land is clear, check your soil's percolation and the nutrients, texture, and acid–alkaline balance [see Soil Percolation Testing, left, and Conducting a Soil Test, opposite]. A percolation test measures how fast your soil drains. Soil texture tests reveal whether your soil is sand, silt, clay, or balanced loam.

Generally, the acidity or alkalinity of your soil is determined by the predominant bedrock. Limestone creates alkaline soil; shale creates acidic soil. Relative acidity affects the ability of plants to absorb nutrients. A pH test measures on a numbered scale with 7.0 neutral, acid indicated by lower numbers, and alkaline by higher numbers. Ideal gardening soil usually has a slightly acidic pH between 6.5 and 7.0, but most perennials will grow at pH levels between 6.0 and 7.5, and some prefer slightly more acidic or alkaline soil.

There are billions of microscopic bacteria and fungi in good garden soil. You can put them to work by furnishing their favorite conditions—moist soil with plenty of organic matter—while avoiding use of synthetic fertilizers and pesticides. As microorganisms flourish in the soil, they improve its structure, make nutrients available to plant roots, keep soil from becoming too acid or alkaline, and, some research indicates, fight off soil-borne disease organisms.

If the plants on your garden site fail to thrive, or if the soil's pH test is below 6.0 or higher than 7.5, you need information that only can be obtained from a professional laboratory's soil test. For the location of a soil testing laboratory, call your local USDA or Agriculture Canada extension office, or inquire at your local nursery or garden center for the recommendation of a laboratory near you.

SOIL PERCOLATION TESTING

This test evaluates how quickly your soil drains. Dig several holes in your planting bed 2 ft. (60 cm) deep, and fill them with water. After the water drains, fill the holes with water again and note how long it takes for the water to drain. Well-drained garden soil drains at 1–2 in. (25–50 mm) per hour. Slower rates indicate poor drainage. Investigate to see if the cause might be clay soil, a layer of hardpan, impermeable rock, or another underground obstruction. If the water level drops quickly, the soil is too sandy.

(Above right) If you have large beds or your garden soil varies between areas, test soil samples from each location.

(Below) Potting soil is usually a mixture of a loosening agent and compost, such as vermiculite.

CONDUCTING A SOIL TEST

You can perform soil tests for texture, nutrients, and pH yourself. Many nurseries and garden centers provide testing services to assess soil and recommend necessary amendments. If you do need a laboratory test for pH, follow the lab's instructions on gathering samples from different parts of your planting area. Mail or bring the sample to the laboratory. To perform soil tests at home, follow these steps:

1 Collect a small amount of moist soil 3–4 in. (75–100 cm) below the soil surface. If you are testing several sites within your garden, be sure to track each location carefully.

2 Check for texture by squeezing the moist soil sample in your fist, then open your hand. If it feels gritty and falls apart when lightly poked, it contains excess sand. If it holds together, push it between thumb and forefinger to make a ribbon of soil. If the ribbon cracks apart before it is ½ in. (13 mm) long, the soil is silty or loamy. If the ribbon holds together for 1 in. (25 mm), the soil is mostly clay.

3 Measure relative nutrients in your soil samples using a home soil test kit available at most garden retailers. Follow package instructions, which vary according to the specific kit.

4 Determine soil acidity or alkalinity using a pH test kit available at most garden retailers. Follow package instructions and use distilled water for accuracy.

5 Electronic meters check soil pH, too. Check accuracy by testing cow's milk, which has a 6.5–7.0 pH, and thoroughly cleaning the probe before testing your sample.

IMPROVING THE SOIL

The magic ingredient for improving the texture of either sandy or clay soils—and promoting beneficial microorganisms and adding nutrients—is an organic soil amendment. These amendments include compost, decomposed manure, aged sawdust, ground bark, peat moss, and agricultural byproducts such as aged cocoa and rice hulls and mushroom compost.

Flowering perennials require a steady supply of nutrients, water, and air to grow, develop buds, and bloom. Improve your soil with amendments to add nutrients, improve texture and drainage, or change its acid-alkaline balance.

To hold moisture and nutrients in sandy soil, use a fine-textured amendment such as peat moss, compost, or aged manure. To loosen clay soil and add air pockets, use a coarse-textured amendment, including ground bark or rice hulls. To lower the pH of an alkaline soil, use an acidic amendment such as peat moss or ground fir bark. To raise the pH of acidic soil, choose an amendment with a high pH, such as mushroom compost or steer manure.

You can raise or lower soil pH temporarily with chemical amendments. Use limestone or wood ashes to raise the pH of an acid soil toward neutral; use elemental sulfur to lower the pH of an alkaline soil. Follow package instructions for amounts of chemicals or rely on the results of a soil test and apply them carefully, mixing the chemicals into the soil and watering well. It may take a year or more to alter the pH 0.5, and the treatment will last 2–4 years. Gypsum, a mixture of sulfur and calcium, helps correct high sodium in soil, often a problem where high mineral—or softened —water is used for irrigation, but isn't helpful in changing pH.

To promote healthy populations of soil microorganisms, dig in compost or organic fertilizer such as alfalfa pellets sold as rabbit feed, cottonseed meal, earthworm castings, or animal manure. When working with manures, use smaller amounts of concentrated, high-nitrogen bat or seabird guano than you would low-nitrogen cow or chicken manure. Some steer manures are high in sodium, which increases alkalinity.

Choose an organic soil amendment that's aged. Fresh manure contains too much nitrogen for most plants, while fresh sawdust and hulls deplete nitrogen as they decompose. Screen the amendment to remove debris and weeds and choose those ground to uniform consistency.

Amendments are available in bulk at landscape material yards and in bags at garden centers. They are sold by the cubic foot (0.03 m³) or cubic yard (0.8 m³). Two cubic feet (0.06 m³) covers 6 square feet (0.6 m²) with a 4-inch (10-cm) layer. One cubic yard (0.8 m³) contains 27 cubic feet (0.8 m³) and covers 80 square feet (7.4 m²) with a 4-inch (10-cm) layer.

Apply fertilizer in a ring around the plant's drip line—it's an imaginary circle drawn beneath the perimeter of the plant's outer foliage. The soil beneath this area contains most of the plant's roots.

PREPARING AND AMENDING SOIL

1 Begin by clearing all weeds and plants you plan to remove. Remove rocks and debris at least 18 in. (45 cm) deep.

Ready soil for planting, add soil amendments, and fertilize by double digging the bed. The soil should be moist, neither soggy wet nor powder dry. Water lightly the evening before you start. Gather together a shovel, tarp, spading fork, rake, tiller, and enough organic soil amendment to cover the area 4-in. (10-cm) deep. While some effort is required, double digging is easy to understand and perform when you follow these steps:

2 Dig a trench 9–12-in. (23–30-cm) deep and one shovel-width wide along an edge of the bed, placing removed soil on a tarp. Loosen the next 9–12 in. (23–30 cm) of soil within the trench with a spading fork or shovel.

3 Widen the trench a second shovel width, placing the top 9–12 in. (23–30 cm) of its soil into the first trench. Progress across the area until all the soil has been dug. Fill the last trench with soil from the first. Use a tiller to thoroughly mix the topsoil.

4 Cover the area with a 4-in. (10-cm) layer of organic soil amendment, as needed. Add synthetic or organic fertilizer, as needed, following package instructions.

5 Turn the soil amendments into the top 9–12 in. (23–30 cm) of soil using a shovel or fork.

6 Rake the top of the bed smooth. It will be high and fluffy with air and amendments; avoid compacting it to retain its texture. Water with a sprinkler and allow it to settle for at least 24 hours before planting.

SITE IMPROVEMENTS

Drip irrigation systems can be fitted with drip emitters that discharge water in a variety of patterns—sprays (top), drip (center), or bubbler (bottom)—and at different flow rates. The combination of options allow you to tailor each outlet to your plant's specific watering needs.

If your garden plan includes adding systems such as drainage, garden lighting, and irrigation, you need to coordinate those tasks with improving the soil. Usually, underground drainage and irrigation pipes are installed before the soil is amended. Generally, low-voltage lighting fixtures are added after planting. If you need help with any site improvements, contact a licensed landscape contractor for help.

Drainage: If your property has runoff or standing water, consult a professional for advice before proceeding. Always build raised beds so they channel runoff away from structures and neighboring yards. If perennial beds are installed adjacent to a house or other building, grade the soil at least 2 inches (50 mm) per 10 feet (3 m) so that water drains away from the structure.

Lighting: Low-voltage lighting kits make garden lighting safe and easy. Ensure that your site has an outlet protected by a ground fault circuit interrupter [GFCI] or ask an electrician to install one; the kit's transformer will plug into this outlet. Shop for a lighting kit with spotlights and floodlights rather than path lights, to focus light on the plants and keep fixtures hidden. After planting, place floodlights where they'll accent your tall plantings: set some near the trunks of shrubs and tall, thin-leafed perennial plants to uplight the canopy. Set other lights at the curves of the bed or border, at the front edge to light up pale flowers or muted foliage, and in the middle to uplight thin, open, or elegantly shaped plants. Check from all vantage points to assure the viewer sees the plants rather than bright or glaring edges from the fixtures. Before connecting fixtures to the 12-volt cable, leave extra cable between them—loop it into a tidy circle at the base of a stake—so the fixtures can be adjusted as the plants grow. Cover the cable with mulch or bury it in the soil.

Irrigation: An automatic irrigation system can be a lifesaver for your plants, especially if you live in a low-rainfall climate, have limited time to water regularly, or travel frequently. There are two basic styles of permanent irrigation systems: high-pressure sprays and low-pressure drips. High-pressure systems are constructed of rigid polyvinyl chloride (PVC) pipe that delivers water to stationary or rotating spray heads. They deliver lots of water—1.5–3 gallons per minute (6–11 lpm)—equivalent to a heavy downpour. A low-pressure drip irrigation system uses flexible polyethylene tubing laid on the soil surface. It delivers water slowly—at rates ranging from 0.5–3 gallons per hour (2–11 lph) —through drip emitters. Drip systems are easier to install and control than sprays and easily can be changed. Both systems use valves mounted to your yard's permanent plumbing. Most include automatic timers to turn the system on and off. Spray heads, rotors, and drip emitters are divided into separate watering "circuits," each on a separate valve, since different outlets require varying lengths of time.

Your choice of drip or spray irrigation depends on your water pressure—spray systems need more than drip systems—and the size and shape of the area to be irrigated. Use sprays in areas measuring 10–15 feet (3–5 m) wide, rotors for areas 15–30 feet (5–10 m) wide, and drip systems for any area size or shape. Sprays deliver too much water for sloping sites or clay soil; rotors and drip make better choices there.

Installing a permanent irrigation system is straightforward and simple, but it must be designed carefully to ensure even coverage. Personalized help is available from hardware retailers, irrigation suppliers, water districts, and extension offices.

INSTALLING IN-GROUND IRRIGATION

Design your system to match your soil, water pressure, and slope. Choose approved backflow prevention valves, and comply with all local code requirements. Locate control valves in an accessible spot near the control timer. In cold-winter areas, use an insulated subsurface enclosure or install it indoors. Locate your spray heads to avoid damage to plants. Follow these steps:

1 Trench from your water entry to the control valve site, to the start point of each watering circuit, and to create each irrigation circuit. Turn off water at the main, then install a gate valve and a backflow prevention valve to isolate the water supply for the irrigation system.

2 Lay schedule 40 PVC pipe to local code from the backflow preventer to the control valves. Install a valve for each circuit. Use a step-down bushing to reduce the line gauge, then install lateral lines to the site of each spray head or emitter.

3 Join pipe sections with couplers, using PVC primer and solvent for slip fittings, Teflon® tape for threaded fittings.

4 Install swing joints or risers at the site of each sprinkler head or drip emitter hose coupler.

5 Flush the system by turning on each valve until the water runs clear, then turning it off again. Install all sprinkler heads or emitter couplers.

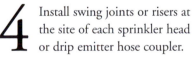

6 Install an automatic control timer. Connect it with direct-buried control cable to the manifold valves. Program the controller and test the system; adjust spray heads as needed. Refill trenches.

RAISED BEDS

Raised planters surrounded by dry-stacked fieldstone or rock boulders are easy to build and work well in natural and casual gardens. Fill the spaces between stones with trailing perennials, and perch taller plants in soil-filled niches atop the rocks.

A raised bed is a gardening dream—a well-drained spot where plants thrive in rich, loose-textured soil [see Preparing and Amending Soil, pg. 35]. Because a raised bed has a soil level 1–2 feet (30–60 cm) above ground, it provides excellent drainage. Filled with ideal soil, it offers plants a rich, nutritious, well-textured environment. Raised beds also offer easier access for care and can be trimmed with bench edges for use as seats while gardening or enjoying the blooming show.

Most raised beds are enclosed by low wooden or simple masonry walls. They easily can be built in a weekend, unlike retaining walls, which require engineering expertise. Select a wall material that reflects the theme of your garden.

Wood is a popular choice for square and rectangular beds. If the bed's walls are 15–18 inches (38–45 cm) tall, the sides of the bed can double as benches by adding a wide plank top. For a formal look, paint the wood and add finials to the posts. For a rustic look, set lengths of split cedar timbers or posts upright at differing heights into the ground. Where soil comes into direct contact with wood, use rot-resistant materials such as cedar, hemlock, redwood, or pressure-treated softwood.

Stone—rounded fieldstone, thin flagstones, or even broken concrete—can be dry stacked into curving walls without mortar, and the joints between stones planted with trailing perennials such as cranesbill, gazania, and lamb's-ears. Mortared bricks create classic raised beds. Use new bricks for formal gardens, used brick for a more casual look. Set them three or four courses high to create a raised bed.

Consider also mortarless wall-building systems, available at many home improvement centers. Most are easy to install and use the block's weight for stability.

The most charming raised beds use whimsical odds and ends. One gardener recycled wine bottles from a restaurant, setting them bottoms-up along a bed. Another set terra-cotta drain pipes to create planting nooks for a collection of jewel-like miniature perennials.

Whatever materials you choose, your raised beds will add visual interest and will be sure to please your perennials.

BUILDING A WOODEN RAISED-BED PLANTER

Before beginning this one-day project, measure the site and sketch your design for the planter, using standard lengths of lumber and avoiding compound angles if possible. In addition to the materials listed, gather together a level, reciprocating saw, drill, screwdriver, and shovel. Follow these simple steps:

1 Use a shovel, rake, and turfing tool to clear the site of turf, plants, weeds, and debris. Level the site.

Required Materials:

4	2×12-in. (38×286-mm)	Side boards
4	4×4-in. (72×72-mm)	Posts
4	2×12-in. (38×286-mm)	Seat top
(Dimension as required for site and project)		
20	⅜×5½-in. (10×140-mm)	Carriage bolts
20	⅜-in. (10-mm)	Nuts & washers
16	⅜×3½-in. (10×90-mm)	Deck screws

2 Measure and mark side boards and posts. Cut side boards and posts to length with a reciprocating saw.

3 Dig postholes at each corner. Install posts, checking for square and level. Mark and drill holes for carriage bolts. Fasten side boards to the posts with bolts before backfilling the postholes.

5 Cut 45° bevels in the seat top boards. Drill holes and fasten them to the posts and side boards with deck screws. Seal the seat top with clear penetrating sealer, or prime and paint the bed's exterior.

4 After the four sides of the planter have been fastened, fill the planter with fertile, well-textured loam or a complete soil replacement.

BUILDING A MAILBOX PLANTER

This weekend project combines building skills and love of flowering perennial plants. In addition to the building materials, visit a salvage yard to find an interesting rectangular planter to suspend below the mailbox. Ours was made of brass with an antique patinae. To build yours, follow these steps:

Required Materials:

1	4×4×96-in. (89×89×2,438-mm)	Post
2	2×4×47-in. (38×89×1,194-mm)	Side rails
2	2×4×10¾-in. (38×89×273-mm)	Spacers
1	2×6×17½-in. (38×140×445-mm)	Box shelf
2	2×8×16½-in. (38×184×419-mm)	Brace
2	1×2×27-in. (19×38×686-mm)	Long frames
2	1×2×6¼-in. (19×38×159-mm)	Short frames
12	1-in. (25 mm) Wooden buttons	
8	Lathe-turned cabinet pulls	
1	Decorative brass cap.	
6	¼×5½-in. (6×140-mm) Bolts, nuts, and washers	
6	#8×2-in. (4×50-mm) Brass wood screws	
16	#6×1½-in. (3.5×40-mm) Brass wood screws	

1 Chisel a mortise channel 3½ in. (89 mm) wide and 14 in. (35 cm) from the end of each side rail, to receive the post and compensate for wood thickness differences.

2 Use a jigsaw to cut an arc 5½ in. (140 mm) in diameter in each end of the brace and arc corners 3 in. (75 mm) in diameter in one end of each side rail. Cut a kerf 2¹¹⁄₁₆ in. long (68 mm) long and ½ in. (12 mm) deep into edge of the side rails at the arc corner.

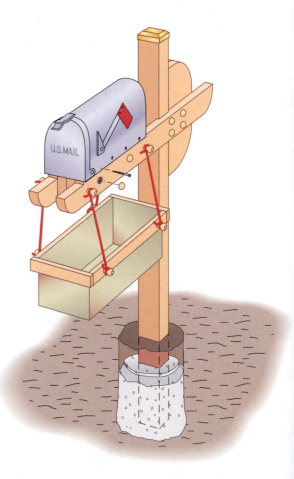

3 On a layout table, assemble, square, and clamp post, side rails, spacers, and brace. Use a 1-in (25-mm) paddle bit to drill 6 holes, ½ in. (13 mm) deep, centered at the site of each bolt. Invert the assembly and repeat on the other side.

4 Use a ⁵⁄₁₆-in. (8-mm) spade bit to through-drill the 6 bolt holes. Fasten the assembly with bolts, washers, and nuts, set finger-tight plus 1½ turns.

5 Use exterior wood glue and a wooden button to plug each bolt hole. Tap the button into place using a soft mallet wrapped with a soft cloth.

6 Drill receiving holes for the cabinet pulls that will support the planter. Use exterior wood glue to fasten the cabinet pulls into the side rails. Glue the decorative cap onto the post.

7 Attach the box shelf to the side rails with 6 #8 wood screws, positioning it flush with the kerf end.

8 Fasten the mailbox to the box shelf with 8 #6 wood screws. Adjust the box position to allow the door to freely open.

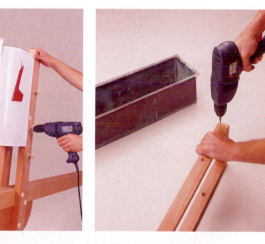

9 Fasten the planter hanging frame with 2 #6 wood screws at each corner. Drill and attach 4 cabinet pulls with wood glue.

10 Fill the planter box with potting soil and plants. Insert the planter box into the support frame and suspend it from the side rails with nylon rope, cord, or chain.

BORDERS AND EDGINGS

Define your in-ground perennial bed with an attractive edging—a low line of brick, stone, concrete, plastic, or wood set along its perimeter. Edgings are usually 6 inches (15 cm) high or less. Select an edging material that coordinates with the garden's look: brick or painted wood for formal gardens, natural stone or aged wood for those with a more casual style, and concrete pavers or bright plastic for modern styling. To coordinate with a natural garden, seek out local materials such as flagstone for a southwestern look or rocks found at the site. Materials that complement your home's architecture also are a good choice.

Edgings add decorative accents and simplify maintenance, too. Crisp rows of brick along that all-important front edge give your beds a tidy appearance even when your plants are dormant. Edgings set along walkways discourage feet from straying into the plants, and beautifully divide beds from lawns or ground cover. Where lawn meets perennial beds, grass must be edged by hand because power string trimmers might damage perennial blooms and foliage. A solid edging allows you to set the canopy of the trimmer against it and work quickly.

To install a brick or paver edging, dig a trench the desired width and depth plus 1 inch (25 mm). Pour 1–2 inches (25–50 mm) of sand in the bottom of the trench. Set the edging materials in place—set bricks and pavers halfway into the ground, either at right angles or on a diagonal, and set fieldstones with one-third of their height underground. Tap them using a rubber-headed mallet for solid placement and to ensure fit. In regions where soil freezes, use grout between pieces.

Constructing masonry edgings provides a permanent and distinctive outline around perennial planting areas [see opposite]. With masonry, you can control the exact shape of the edging to precisely match your garden plan.

For additional convenience, install mow strips between your edging and lawn. Mow strips are paving or masonry set at soil level where turf and planting bed meet. They're sufficiently wide for a mower wheel to traverse, edging the lawn as you mow.

Edging choices have expanded to prefabricated wood, plastic, and metal options that can be installed in minutes to create a neat look around your perennial beds and borders.

CONSTRUCTING MASONRY EDGING

Working with concrete allows you many options for the edging's shape, color, and pattern. To add interest, texture the concrete using split shingle forms or brush the concrete as it dries, add color tints, or press in stones for surface decoration. Gather together a straight-edged shovel, hammer, benderboard for forms, a bundle of stakes, nails, mixing trough for concrete, and a spade. To build the forms and pour the concrete, follow these steps:

1 Mark the edge using flour or string. Dig a trench along the edge of the bed or border 6 in. (30 cm) deep using a straight-edge trenching shovel.

2 Position the form boards on each side of trench. Forms should be 1 in. (25 mm) from the bottom and sides of the trench. Square and level the tops of the forms.

3 Support the form boards with a 1×2-in. (19×38-mm) stake spaced approximately 2 feet (60 cm) apart. Nail diagonally into a sledge to clinch them.

4 Mix the concrete according to its bag instructions. Shovel concrete to fill forms to the top using the shovel to vibrate and settle it into the form's sides and bottom.

5 Move a striker board across the top of the form, filling hollows, removing any excess concrete, and making the surface roughly level.

6 After the water of formation is absorbed and while the concrete is still workable, use a steel edging tool to finish the edges along the form. At 4-ft. (1.2-m) intervals, crease the concrete to provide control joints. If desired, add surface texture effects. Dry overnight.

Perennials are offered as seeds and potted specimens in varying sizes. This chapter provides information to help you select healthy perennials and plant them correctly into the landscape: in formal and casual designs, in containers, and in-ground.

Visit plant nurseries and garden centers in your area. Look for grounds that are neat and tidy, plants that look healthy, and staff who are both courteous and knowledgeable. In some locales, the nursery industry provides education: look for people wearing a certified nursery professional badge.

The best time to shop for plants is late in the week, after wholesale growers have made their deliveries of fresh plants to the garden center or nursery but before the weekend shopping rush begins. Allow ample time for shopping, thorough inspection of plants, and making your plant selections. Be sure to bring your garden plan and your plant list for reference.

Look in your area for specialty nurseries that focus on certain plants. If you're planning a perennial garden with a specific planting theme—local natives, butterfly-attracting plants, drought-tolerant plants, or aquatic plants for water gardens —these stores often have a wider though more specialized selection than general nurseries. Their owners and staff often are passionate about their interests and happy to share their experience and knowledge with you.

Direct retailers offer plants, especially unusual varieties and regional specialties that general retailers lack. Many have electronic catalogs and will respond to your queries. When ordering plants from sources located in different USDA plant hardiness zones than your own, always check the plant's suitability for your climate and garden.

Seek out special sales through community garden clubs, botanical gardens, and native plant societies. These nonprofit organizations provide unusual plants suited to the region, and knowledgeable gardeners usually are on hand to answer questions.

> With garden planning and preparation complete, begin choosing plants and setting them in place in your garden

Planting a Perennial Garden

Water recently acquired perennial plants the evening before you plant them in the garden. Many plants have grown to fill their nursery containers and may be root bound. Use a hand fork to loosen the rootball and untangle any encircling roots before planting the perennial.

SELECTING PERENNIALS

Flowering perennials usually are sold in standard sizes: 1-gallon (4-l) containers, 4-inch (10-cm) containers, and in so-called six-packs, either small or jumbo size. The larger plants make an instant show in the garden, but the economical smaller container plants will catch up within three months of good growing weather. Because the rootball is small in six-packs, these plants require an entire growing season to match the larger options.

The proper appearance for perennials growing in nursery containers is short and stocky; avoid plants that are tall and lanky. The short plants have room to spare in their nursery containers and become established more quickly in the garden than taller counterparts.

Growth should be uniform throughout the plant; for plants that sprout directly from the soil, examine the number of stems or growing points: more points mean a bigger plant. Avoid plants with signs of physical damage such as broken stems or leaves.

Check that leaves are firm, spring back to place when touched, and are deeply colored without a yellow or purple taint, which may indicate nutritional deficiencies or overwatering. Look for signs of insect damage, such as chewed holes and disease indications including the gray powdering and deformed leaves of powdery mildew.

Since the long-term growth potential of a perennial resides in its roots, examine them carefully. The topsoil surface should be free of roots. Drainage holes on the bottom should reveal only a few root hairs. If many surface roots are visible or many subsurface roots are growing out of the drainage holes, check further. Gently compress the sides of the plastic container and, with a hand over the soil surface to support the plant's stem, turn the container upside down, and slide the container from the plant. The rootball should show firm, white roots that loosely fill the pot. Reject plants with a mat of tangled roots or ones that are brownish or decayed. When buying perennials in smaller containers, avoid all that are root bound. Inspect perennials in six-packs and reject any with roots in a spongy cube that resists compression. Since perennials have large, fast-growing root systems, once their progress is stalled, many will fail to regain their vigor.

Perennials also can be started from seed. Growing from seed is much more economical than acquiring nursery plants. This method requires patience waiting for perennials to bloom and regular care as the seedlings mature. Read seed packets carefully for planting guidelines and care needs.

Choose perennials that have received constant, proper care while at the grower's nursery and in the garden store:

(Top) Avoid plants with yellowed or purple foliage discolorations that may indicate improper watering or fertilizing.

(Center) Pass by plants that have broken stems or torn leaves, choosing those with stocky, healthy growth.

(Bottom) Slip the plant out of its container and examine its roots: plants should show fine hair roots throughout the rootball, without signs of withering or matted growth.

Healthy plants have abundant, well-formed leaves with rich green coloration, flower bud development, and vigorous trunk and hair roots.

CHOOSING HEALTHY PLANTS

Take time and ask questions when plant shopping. Ask store personnel if the nursery or garden center stocks perennials in various sizes. Often plants are grouped according to container size, rather than species. Carefully check plant labels against your plant list for correct names and varieties, since many species appear similar when out of bloom. Verify mature heights and bloom colors against your garden plan as you browse:

1 Look at the overall shape of the plant. Choose those with short, sturdy growth. Pick plants with uniform growth and with several strong growth points in the crown. Avoid those with broken stems or leaves.

2 Check leaves for deep color and signs of diseases or pests. Avoid plants with faded, yellow, mottled, or discolored leaves.

3 Examine the bottom of the container to see if roots are visible or growing out of drainage holes. Avoid such plants that have been held too long in their containers.

4 Compress the sides of the container and, supporting the top of the rootball with one hand, upend the container. Slip out the plant to evaluate the roots; they should be firm, white, and have ample space for growth.

GOOD PLANTING PRACTICES

Perennial flowers quickly grow to mature size, filling the bed or border with profuse blooms. Space your plants to avoid crowding and ensure proper air circulation and sunlight.

Get your plants off to a great start by planting them with care. Take care of yourself as well by wearing work gloves, protective clothing, and sunscreen when gardening to avoid hazard from abrasion and the sun's strong ultraviolet rays.

When you first bring container plants home from the nursery or garden center, set them in a semishady location and water immediately. Promptly open shipping boxes from direct merchants and follow the grower's instructions prior to planting.

The best time to plant is during cool weather in spring and autumn. Check local weather forecasts, and schedule planting for cool overcast days without frost. In warmer seasons, plant in late afternoon to avoid the stress of noon sun. Water all plants and the planting area thoroughly the day before you intend to plant.

Before installing individual plants for a bed, border, or entire garden, do a practice placement to confirm your design. Begin by transferring the measurements on your garden plan to the ground. Set plants in their nursery containers at the

planting site. If some plants are missing, substitute a short bamboo stake as a placeholder. This will be your final opportunity to adjust the design before the plants are installed. Arrange individual plants for bloom color and height. Verify mature growth width when you combine plants in a bed or border. Preview your design by walking around the planting area and viewing it from every angle, including from inside the house.

Once you're satisfied with your final design, begin digging. Installing an entire garden is a process of repeating the correct planting procedures for individual plants. Start at the back of the border or the center of beds and work with larger plants first.

The depth of your hole is very important to the success of your plants. Regardless of the size of the plant, dig the hole to make sure that the top of the rootball is level with the soil's surface. When it is lower, water puddles around the plant's crown to promote fungal disease. In heavily amended soil, create planting holes somewhat shallower than the depth of the rootball because the soil will settle after watering.

After digging the hole, add fertilizer [see Fertilizers, pg. 62]. Use a complete organic or synthetic dry fertilizer labeled 10–10–10, meaning it contains 10 percent by weight of nitrogen, phosphorus, and potassium, the three most important plant nutrients. Adding them to soil at the sides of the rootball where roots will grow first ensures that plants will have nutrients when they start growing.

Once the plants are installed, water them using a hose-end sprayer filled with a half-strength solution of water and foliar fertilizer. This helps settle the soil and provides quick uptake nutrients to help the plants offset transplant shock.

After the plants are in place and the soil is settled, perform the final steps to ensure your plants get off to a healthy start. Place drip irrigation emitters [see Installing a Simple Drip Irrigation System, pg. 59]. Add stakes and supports as needed, positioning them outside the rootball, and tie the stems. Collect the plant labels and save them so you'll remember each plant.

Rustic rail fences, stone walls, and other casual elements work best in gardens that are designed to match a home's informal style. For contemporary homes, or those with regular geometric features, choose more formal fences, walls, and paths.

Rake protective mulch around the plants to stop weeds from germinating, lessen evaporation, and moderate soil temperature changes [see Organic Mulches, pg. 64]. Keep a circle free of mulch around the plant's stem in order to avoid fungal spores and help stems quickly dry.

Be sure to water your new plantings regularly until they are established. Your plants also may need protection as they adjust to their new home. They likely were held in a semishady nursery and will wilt in hot sun unless protected with a sunshade.

CONTAINERS FOR PERENNIALS

When choosing containers for perennials, go big. Usually, only a pot at least 14 inches (35 cm) in diameter has room for the roots of a vigorous perennial. For mixed plantings, larger sizes allow you to mix plants.

Select containers with drain holes to provide proper drainage. Prevent soil from sifting from drain holes by placing plastic screening over them before adding soil. For containers on concrete or other paving, place a catch basin beneath to catch drips that might stain. On wooden decks and porches, raise the container and saucer off the surface, using decorative pot feet or a plant stand, allowing air to circulate and avoiding standing water.

Soil for containers must drain well, yet retain moisture. Start with potting mix. For plants that need moist conditions, add compost or peat moss to the potting soil; for plants that require well-drained soil, add perlite, lava rock, and builders' sand to the mix. Homemade compost is ideal for customizing soil for your plants. To help hold water, add water-holding plastic polymers to the potting soil [see Watering Devices, pg. 60].

Plant containers densely when combining several plants in one pot. Space root-balls ½ inch (13 mm) apart. To place more plants, reform cubic 4-inch (10-cm) rootballs by gently pressing their sides so the rootball becomes longer than wide.

Fertilize container plants with a complete, balanced, liquid or dry organic fertilizer, or choose a time-release encapsulated granule fertilizer [see Fertilizers, pg. 62].

Brick paths lined with container perennials add color and create interest in an entry. The bricks' hard texture contrasts nicely with the softness of blooms and foliage.

Choose a color, style, and material that complements your home's architecture, display site, or garden theme: terra cotta for rustic and country styles, cast concrete or fiberglass classic decorations for more formal architecture, colorfully glazed pots for contemporary or tropical looks, and natural wood planters for casual styles.

PLANTING IN CONTAINERS

Water your plants the day before planting. They should be moist but avoid sogginess. If you're using water-holding polymers, soak them in water until plump before mixing into the soil. In addition to the plants, gather together the container, hand trowel, piece of screening if desired, soil mix, fertilizers, and a watering can. Follow these steps:

2 Compress the nursery container and, cupping the top of the rootball in your palm, upend the container and slip out the plant. Free any entwined roots.

1 Put a piece of screen in the bottom of the container. Fill the container with potting soil to a depth of the longest rootballs plus 1 in. (25 mm). Final soil level will be 1 in. (25 mm) below container rim. Lightly compress soil with your fingers.

3 Beginning with your largest plants, set the plants on the soil in the container. Gently compress the sides of rootballs to rectangular form. Add soil to the depth of the next longest rootballs plus 1 in. (25 mm).

4 Repeat the process with each group of smaller plants. Loosen roots at the side of each rootball and place the plants approximately ½ in. (13 mm) apart.

5 Thoroughly water plants and soil with a half-strength solution of liquid fertilizer in a watering can, following package instructions for new plantings. Add more soil if needed. The tops of the rootballs should show slightly on the soil surface.

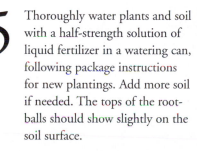

INSTALLING PERENNIAL GARDENS

1 Once you have obtained your plants, verify individual specimens on your garden plan. Transfer the measurements from your garden plan to your planting area.

As you plan for planting day, allow sufficient time to set in each specimen properly—you'll avoid undue exertion and your plants will get off to a fine start. Divide large areas into manageable sections. Water your plants the day before planting. They should be moist but avoid sogginess. In addition to your plants, gather together your garden plan, a yardstick, a shovel or border spade, a hand trowel, a hand fork, granular and liquid fertilizers, a hose-end sprayer, organic mulch, and a rake. Follow these easy steps:

2 In a properly prepared and amended planting area, set out nursery containers according to your garden plan. Use a yardstick to space plants correctly. Mark locations of missing plants with bamboo stakes.

3 View the planting area from all sides, including your house. For formal designs, blend plant combinations smoothly into the whole, match groups symmetrically, and create crisp edges. Adjust as necessary.

4 For casual designs, make sure that plants are balanced, that tall accents lead the eye through the planting, and that there are no squared-off edges, straight lines, or accidental symmetry. Adjust as necessary.

TRANSPLANTING FROM NURSERY CONTAINERS

If you're planting perennials in unimproved soil around existing trees or shrubs, dig the planting hole 2–3 times as wide as the nursery container and 18 inches (45 cm) deep. Add amendments to the removed soil and backfill to the proper planting depth so the new plant will be surrounded with improved soil. Use care to avoid disturbing existing roots. To plant perennials from nursery containers into a bed or border, follow these steps:

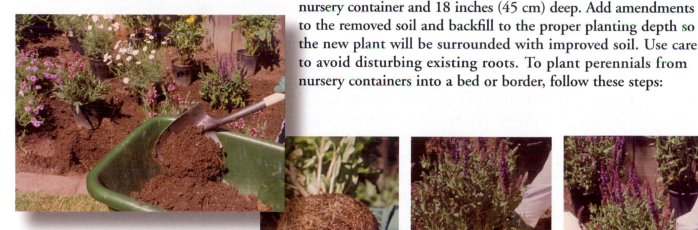

1 Once you're satisfied with your bed's design, begin digging. For each plant, dig a hole that is 1½ times as wide and as deep as the plant's rootball.

2 Gently remove the plant from the nursery container. Check the roots: if they fill the rootball, loosen using your fingers or a hand fork.

3 Set the plant in the hole. If the soil is undisturbed, place the top of the rootball even with surrounding soil. In loose, amended soil, set it above nearby soil.

4 Fill the hole halfway with soil. Firm the soil lightly using your fingers. Sprinkle complete fertilizer on the soil around the rootball, avoiding the roots, following package instructions for new plantings.

5 Fill the hole with soil to the top of the plant's rootball. Thoroughly water both plants and soil with a half-strength solution of liquid fertilizer in a hose-end sprayer, following all package instructions for new plantings.

6 Adjust drip irrigation lines so emitters are on the rootball, but not near the stem or crown, and pin in place. Install supports if needed.

7 Allow the soil to settle. Add 2 in. (50 mm) of organic mulch in a layer around each plant. Keep mulch at a distance of at least 3 in. (75 mm) away from stems.

COMBINING BULBS WITH PERENNIALS

Plants that grow from bulbs—including true bulbs, corms, rhizomes, and tubers—are natural companions for flowering perennials. Bulbs provide color when perennials are dormant, especially in the early spring. Their flowers and foliage are distinctive in the landscape and supply interesting textural contrast in containers.

For the best effect, plant bulbs in groups, numbering at least 10 for tulips and daffodils, and three for lilies. In a formal border, locate bulbs in matched groupings or march them through a bed or along the front of the border. In informal gardens, plant bulbs in irregular masses. Check mature plant heights in mixed plantings.

To ensure that bulbs grow and bloom year after year, plant varieties that suit your climate. Many bulbs have been cultivated for cold climates. Select bulbs that are plump and firm, without soft or discolored spots. Store them in a cool, dry place before planting. Spring-blooming bulbs generally are planted in autumn of the year prior to first bloom; plant summer-blooming bulbs in spring as soon as the soil has warmed and can be worked.

Plant bulbs in well-drained soil amended with compost. Plant bulbs at the proper depth for the species [see Bulb Planting Depths, below]. Check the grower's instructions for other popular tubers and rhizomes.

Spring bulbs make their showy presence known while perennials are just beginning to sprout. In a few months, the foliage of tulips, iris, and narcissus will fade beneath the perennials.

Fertilize bulbs at planting and again each autumn using a complete fertilizer that is low in nitrogen and high in potash such as a 5–10–20 formula [see Fertilizers, pg. 62]. Water after planting and when bulbs are in active growth.

After the flowers fade, cut off seed pods and allow the foliage to turn yellow before trimming so bulbs can store energy for next year's flowers. In regions with freezing winters, lift tender plants such as tuberous begonias after the first frost and store them in a cool, dry place for the winter.

BULB PLANTING DEPTHS

Use these depths for planting in well-amended and textured loam. To plant in other soil types, dig a wider and deeper hole, amend the soil before planting, and backfill to the proper depth before you place the bulb into the hole.

- Dahlias   6 inches (15 cm)
- Daffodils   6–7 inches (15–18 cm)
- Gladiolus   4–6 inches (10–15 cm)
- Iris   4–6 inches (10–15 cm)
- Lilies   6–9 inches (15–23 cm)
- Tulips   8–10 inches (20–25 cm)

PLANTING PERENNIAL BULBS, CORMS, AND TUBERS

Plant spring-blooming bulbs in autumn, after the soil 6 inches (15 cm) below the surface cools to 60°F (15°C) and before the surface soil freezes. Plant summer-blooming bulbs after the soil warms in spring. Mark your bulb plantings with a plant label or bamboo stake at each site and indicate them for reference on your garden plan. To plant bulbs, gather together a border spade or bulb planter, hand trowel, plant labels, granular fertilizer with a 5–10–20 formula, and follow these steps:

2 Place fertilizer in bottom of hole, following package instructions for type of bulb. Cover fertilizer with 1 in. (25 mm) of soil to prevent bulb contact.

1 In a prepared area of amended soil, dig holes to the package recommended depth plus 2 in. (50 mm), and slightly wider than the bulb's diameter. For lilies, dig holes 6 in. (15 cm) deeper than required. Fill lily holes with 6 in. (15 cm) of compost.

3 Set the bulb into the hole, rounded root end down, pointed end up. Set tubers or corms with sprouts up. If you're unsure of the top, plant the tubers or corms lying on their sides.

4 Loosely pack soil around the bulb, fill the hole with soil, and then compact it using your hands. Water thoroughly.

5 Apply a loose mulch to insulate the bulbs from temperature fluctuations and freeze-thaw cycles.

O nce established, most perennial plants thrive with little more than basic care. Daily to weekly maintenance for flowering perennials includes watering regularly, clipping spent blooms, and weeding. Seasonal care includes amending their soil as needed through fertilizing and mulching. Yearly gardening maintenance includes performing a garden tune-up at the start of the blooming season; dividing crowded plants to propagate new plants at the end of the season; and providing winter protection for delicate specimens. Extra care may be needed if garden pests invade or diseases infect your garden. This chapter presents easy instructions for executing each of these gardening tasks.

Early each spring, give your perennial garden a complete tune-up, preparing it for seasonal growth and bloom. The tune-up—pruning, weeding, amending, fertilizing, cultivating, watering, and mulching—makes your garden healthy and beautiful for another season. If you garden in a mild climate—USDA plant hardiness zones 8–11 —you should repeat the tune-up process in late July for blooms into autumn.

Begin your tune-up by pruning dead or decaying foliage and faded flower stems on perennial plants. Pull weeds, using a weeding fork for those with deep roots and fingers for shallow-rooted ones. Also rake weeds and clippings from the soil surface and toss pest- and disease-free foliage into your compost pile. Working in a small area, top off the soil with an inch (25 mm) of amendment such as organic compost or well-rotted manure. Add a complete fertilizer, either an organic or synthetic product. Using a small shovel or hand trowel, turn soil over 2–3 inches (50–75 mm), mixing in amendments and fertilizer. Avoid plant stems or crowns, work from the back of the border to the front to limit soil compacting, and keep the soil loose and fluffy. Thoroughly water your garden after fertilizing.

> **Perennials are long-lived, permanent plants that repay your care by growing and flowering every year**

Caring for Flowering Perennials

Proper irrigation of perennials means regular waterings whenever their surrounding soil becomes dry. Avoid over-watering. Use a hand trowel to check the soil's moistness beneath the surface; if it is still wet, delay watering until it dries completely.

WATERING

How much water do plants need, and when do they need it? The answers are, it depends. Your timing and the amount of water to apply depend on weather conditions, your soil, and your specific plants. Plants need more water in hot and windy weather and less on cool, still days. Plants growing in sandy soil should be watered more often than those growing in heavy clay. Water your moisture-loving plants more frequently, and let drought-tolerant varieties dry completely between waterings.

The best time to water is early in the morning, once temperatures begin to rise. This prevents plants from drying out in midday heat, allows foliage to dry completely before evening cool, and discourages slugs and snails.

Always water perennials thoroughly so their roots penetrate deeply rather than limiting their growth to the surface soil. Your goal when watering most perennial plants should be to apply 1 inch (25 mm) of water at the rate it is absorbed, moisten the top 1 foot (30 cm) of soil and plant roots, then allow the soil to dry before watering again so air can penetrate. Properly cultivated and amended soil will provide plants an ideal balance of moisture and air [see Preparing and Amending Soil, pg. 35].

Before watering again, dig 3–4 inches (75–100 mm) down into the soil to assure that it's dry. It's time to water again when the substrate soil feels dry and crumbly, leaving no residue on your hands.

With practice, you'll recognize your garden's watering needs. Soon after planting, water for a set length of time, perhaps 30 minutes. Wait 24 hours and dig a hole 1 foot (30 cm) deep in the bed, away from plant roots, using weeding tool or a trowel. If the soil is dry 1 foot (30 cm) down, water for a longer period; if soggy, water for a shorter period. Adjust the time as necessary for different seasons and weather. New transplants need extra water; if a newly planted rootball is too dense to absorb water, poke a few holes in its top to increase penetration.

Overhead watering should be performed early in the day, only when temperatures will be warm. Damp foliage is susceptible to fungal disease in cool, moist conditions. Water early to allow the plants to quickly dry after watering. Avoid overhead waterings in the evening.

Hose-end diffusers are useful for applying water to the soil around the base of a perennial while avoiding erosion damage.

INSTALLING A SIMPLE DRIP IRRIGATION SYSTEM

An above-ground drip irrigation system eases your maintenance task of watering by saving you time. It also conserves water by slowly emitting the correct amount to each plant, allowing for good absorption and limiting runoff. Create drip systems quickly and inexpensively by attaching battery-controlled timers and filters to nearby hose bibs. A single circuit can water over 100 plants, depending on your water pressure. Check garden centers for advice and follow these simple instructions:

Required Components:
A   Couplers and fittings
B   Drip irrigation water filter and pressure reducer
C   Battery-operated valve, timer, and backflow preventer
D   ¼-in. (6-mm) drip lines
E   Drip emitters
F   Line-placement stakes

1 Couple the valve assembly to the hose bib, then install an in-line water filter to help prevent clogged lines and a pressure reducer. Adapters may be needed where threads don't match exactly.

2 From the filter, attach the supply tubing. This large-diameter tubing carries water to the individual drip lines. It may have several joints and junctions, depending on your garden. Follow manufacturer's instructions for maximum length of each line of tubing.

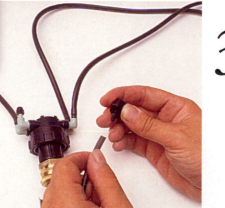

3 Flush the supply tubing. Wherever a drip line is needed, punch a hole in the supply line. Use an adapter to attach a drip line and an emitter for each perennial, choosing ½ gph (2 lph), 1 gph (3.8 lph), or 2 gph (7.6 lph). Stake tubing and lines securely. After planting, cover with mulch.

WATERING DEVICES

Portable watering devices supplement seasonal rainfall. Different methods and equipment suit varied plants and planting situations. For beds, use soaker hoses or lawn sprinklers. For containers, use a hand-held watering wand or watering can.

For the most part, water the ground around the plant rather than its foliage. Water the soil at the plant's natural drip line—a rough circle around the plant where rainfall would drip from leaves. The plant's hair roots are located there, ready to absorb the water. If you grow evergreen perennials in drier climates, gently spray both sides of the leaves once a month with water to discourage populations of thrips and spider mites.

Soaker hoses are specialized portable hoses with tiny holes along their length that either weep or spray. They spread water in narrow or wide corridors throughout a long planting area. Connect them to your hose bib directly or extend them from a garden hose. Their horizontal design makes them a good choice for watering perennial borders.

Impulse pressure sprinklers are cyclical devices that connect to garden hoses and circle in an arc. Place them on a riser 3 feet (90 cm) high to water foliage in a wide area during the mid-morning hours, simulating rain.

Rotating arm sprinklers connect to your standard garden hose. Mount them on stakes to cover the edge and center of planting areas. Position several or move one about every 30 minutes to water the entire area.

A hand-held extension watering wand has fine holes in its rose, or spray nozzle. It is best used for watering container plants, which require more frequent watering than in-ground plants.

A good hand-held watering can is ideal for delivering a measured amount of water, for mixing and delivering water-soluble fertilizers, for watering container perennials, for providing extra water to an individual plant within a planting area, and for watering plants that are otherwise difficult to reach.

Hand watering, while somewhat time-consuming, provides you the opportunity to inspect your plants and to note how your soil is absorbing moisture. As you water, check for signs of pests and disease, the need for deadheading or pruning, and for other changes in your plants. Remember to inspect the undersides of all leaves. Hand watering also provides you a chance to enjoy being outdoors in your garden on a regular basis.

(Left) A watering can with a diffusing rose, or nozzle, is the right choice for watering small-space gardens.

(Below) Water-conservation polymers are soil additives that plump up when watered, then slowly release their moisture to the plants' roots. Use them in your container plantings to avoid dehydration. Also check the soil moisture before each watering.

Water-Conservation Polymers. Polymer granules are more of a water-saving mechanism than an actual watering device. Water-retaining plastic polymers reduce the amount of water you use and the time required for care. Soak these little white nuggets in water and watch them swell as they absorb moisture. Then add them to the soil in your containers, where they will release moisture slowly. Polymers soak up water with each watering, expanding to many times their original size. Soil amended with polymers will stay moist longer than other soil. This is especially helpful for containers because contained soil dries out faster than soil in the ground. Soak polymers in water until plump, then mix them into the soil below the surface 2–3 inches (50–75 mm). When you do water, apply extra water to polymer-amended soil to fill the polymers as well as water the plants.

FERTILIZERS

Plants need nutrients to grow and thrive, just as humans do. The three major nutrients plants need most are nitrogen, phosphorus, and potassium; each must be in its water-soluble form if plants are to absorb them.

Nitrogen, in the form of nitrate salts, is used heavily by plants and soil microorganisms. In excess, it promotes foliage at the expense of blooms. It must be replenished often, since it is carried through the soil with water and is quickly depleted. Phosphorus persists in the soil, but it must be dug down where roots can access it. Potassium leaches with water in all soils but clay. Other micronutrients such as calcium, magnesium, iron, and zinc are sometimes included in fertilizer blends and should be added when soils are deficient.

Fertilizers come in many forms, both organic and synthetic. Typical options include foliar fertilizer that feeds plants as it is absorbed through their leaves, liquid fertilizer such as fish emulsion, and dry meals, manures, and granules.

When choosing fertilizers, ignore labels that imply intended use such as "flower and shrub food" and look at the package label. Most have three numbers—10–10–10 or 0–20–20—that tell the percentage found in the product, by weight, of nitrogen, phosphorus, and potassium in that order. Fertilizers with all three nutrients are called complete fertilizers; those with equal amounts of all three are called balanced fertilizers. Synthetic fertilizers are manmade. Organic fertilizers mean those that are made from decayed plant and animal matter. All types of fertilizers come in many forms:

So-called "starter fertilizers" usually have less nitrogen by percentage of weight than they do phosphorus or potassium. Using them avoids early foliage growth as your perennials' roots become established.

Synthetic granular fertilizers: Economical and widely available, granular fertilizers are used in planting beds or containers, especially as starter fertilizer for new plants.

Encapsulated synthetic and organic fertilizers: Coated with a resin or soluble sulfur, these capsules release nutrients over a long period of time, usually 3–9 months. They are ideal for container plantings.

Liquid organic and synthetic fertilizers: Because the nutrients already are mixed in water, they are ready for easy absorption. These are convenient when applied to the soil or sprayed on foliage for a quick pickup, but always supplement sprays with solid fertilizers for a sustained supply of nutrients.

Spikes and tablets: These concentrated sources of chemical fertilizer are so strong that they sometimes damage plant roots; use them with caution.

Solid organic fertilizers: There are a host of naturally occurring products that provide nutrients. Some are animal in origin including manure and bloodmeal, others are vegetable such as cottonseed meal and alfalfa pellets. Manure should be decomposed and aged before use to avoid burning plants with too much nitrogen and urea. Any packaged manure sold at nurseries and garden centers has been aged and is ready to use. Organic fertilizers improve soil texture and promote the growth of soil organisms, from microbes to earthworms. Most are less concentrated and slower acting than synthetic fertilizers.

FERTILIZING PERENNIALS

Fertilize when installing new plants and when plants break dormancy in spring. Then fertilize halfway through the growing season. Applying fertilizer near the end of the growing season encourages new growth, which easily can be damaged by frost. Always measure amounts carefully—too much fertilizer will harm plants. Apply granular and encapsulated fertilizers at the plant's drip line, the circle following the edge of the plant's foliage. Water your plants well right after fertilizing. Wear protective gloves when handling fertilizers, and follow these steps for various fertilizer forms:

Granular Fertilizer

1 Apply a complete granular fertilizer according to package directions. Measure carefully and apply it to the soil surface.

2 Sprinkle granules on the soil, in a circular pattern beneath the edge of the plant's drip line. Use a hand fork or cultivator to mix fertilizer into the top 2 in. (50 mm) of soil. Water thoroughly to dilute it.

Encapsulated Fertilizer

1 Apply an encapsulated fertilizer according to its package directions, measuring it carefully.

2 Sprinkle encapsulated fertilizer on the soil surface at the plant's drip line. Use a trowel or hand fork to mix the fertilizer into the top 2 in. (50 mm) of soil. Water thoroughly immediately after application.

Liquid Fertilizer

1 Dilute liquid fertilizer as its package directs, then apply over the plant's root zone. Water-soluble foliar fertilizers are absorbed directly by the leaves. Apply both types with a hose-end sprayer. Fertilize on wind-free days cooler than 85° F (29°C).

Solid Fertilizer

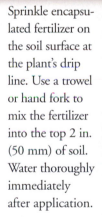

1 To apply solid organic fertilizers, spread a layer of fertilizer ½ in. (13 mm) deep around the base of plants. Work the fertilizer into the soil.

ORGANIC MULCHES

In addition to organic fertilizers, there are organic mulches. Organic fertilizers are decomposed, once-live products that supply nutrients when applied in moderate quantities and worked into the soil [see Fertilizers, pg. 62]. Organic mulches are naturally occurring products that are applied in greater quantities than fertilizers and left in a blanketing layer on top of the soil.

Mulch is one of the best green thumb secrets: it lessens the need for weeding, conserves water, insulates to avoid soil temperature swings, and fortifies the plants. Applied after planting, a layer of mulch keeps weed seeds from germinating; it also reduces watering by slowing evaporation and keeping the surface from forming a dry crust that promotes runoff. In summer, mulch keeps roots cool; in autumn, it delays freezing, allowing roots more growing time; and in winter, it retains cold to prevent plants from heaving out of the ground in thaws. Most of all, organic mulch breaks down as it decays into rich, fragrant humus, creating ideal garden soil without any more effort on your part.

A variety of materials—waste wood chips, bark chips, cocoa hulls, nut hulls, and weed-free straw—are collectively called mulch. For economy, choose a mulch of locally available material. Call an arborist or a tree care company to ask for their waste wood chips. Many types of mulch are available at nurseries and garden centers.

Make organic mulch by composting. Compost, or decomposed organic matter, is an excellent soil amendment and mulch. To compost, gather garden refuse, dried leaves, lawn clippings, and vegetable kitchen refuse—including nutshells and coffee grounds—and store it a covered container until it decomposes. There are a variety of composting systems available at home and garden centers. Compost for mulch is also available at garden centers and nurseries, as well as many other retail stores.

In autumn, collect fallen leaves to serve as a natural winter mulch. Living organic mulch is another option, depending on your garden design. To provide living mulch, grow annual ground covers beneath your flowering perennials. When thriving, the ground cover will act to suppress weeds. After they fade, they will help fortify the soil for the next season.

Inorganic mulch such as gravel, rock, and seashells also will suppress weeds and insulate the ground. Consider inorganic mulches for those locations where you want to block all vegetative growth, including paths through a garden. They also suit some landscape designs, such as a gravel flooring for a few perennials highlighted within an Asian-themed formal garden.

Choices for mulch used in your garden to retain soil moisture, insulate plant roots from temperature fluctuations, block weed growth, and provide supplemental nutrients include (clockwise from top left) cocoa hulls, wood chips, organic compost, ground bark, and straw.

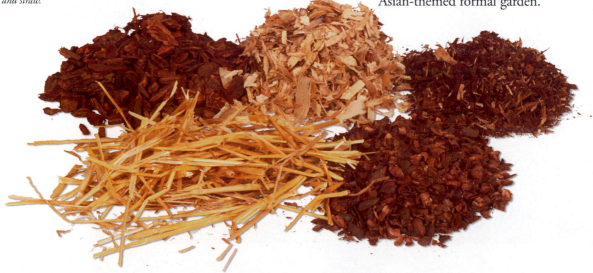

APPLYING ORGANIC MULCH

In autumn or spring, apply mulch around your perennials in a layer 1–3 in. (25–75 mm) deep: less for finely textured materials such as homemade compost, more for coarser materials such as wood chips. A 2-cu. ft. (0.06 m³) bag covers 8 sq. ft. (0.7 m²) to a depth of 3 in. (75 mm). One cubic yard (0.8 m³) covers 100 sq. ft. (9 m²) to a depth of 3 in. (75 mm). To apply mulch, follow these steps:

1 After watering thoroughly, stage evenly spaced piles of organic mulch between perennial plants. Here a coco hull mulch is being used. It is both natural and gives off a rich chocolate aroma. Be sure to check your mulch before application, make sure that it is free of mold or other fungus.

2 Use a leaf or hand rake to spread 1–3 in. (25–75 mm) of mulch evenly around plants.

3 After the planting area is covered, clear the area around each plant. Leave at least 1 in. (25 mm) clear around the stem of each perennial plant.

PESTS AND DISEASES

Once you cultivate a perennial garden, many creatures—birds, insects, mollusks, arachnids, and amphibians—will move in to enjoy it with you. The vast majority are not interested in chewing on your plants, and many of them dine on those that do. As the gardener, you are the manager, the referee, and the host of this open-air carnival of life that is your garden's ecologic balance.

Pest and disease control begins with choosing plants that are suitable to your plant hardiness zone, growing conditions, site, and soil type. Select disease-resistant cultivars, and plant them in soil enriched with manure or compost to boost the population of helpful micro-organisms. Healthy plants usually shrug off insect attacks, bugs, and disease.

Many diseases such as various mildews and fungi are aggravated by undesirable practices such as overhead watering late in the day. When disease strikes, immediately remove the damaged foliage and discard it to avoid spreading spores.

Become acquainted with the most common insect pests and their predators, what they eat, and when to expect them. Even beneficial insects can look ferocious such as the orange-and-black beaded skin of ladybug larvae, a voracious predator of aphids.

As a good host, offer beneficial creatures shelter in rocks and leaf litter, a water source, and nectar and pollen plants to sip when not attacking pests. Many beneficial insects are tiny and need small flowers such as those of yarrow or the compound flowers of cosmos and daisies. Provide nectar sources from early spring to late autumn to attract and hold these garden friends.

When you first notice insect damage, wait before quick use of a pesticide. Remember that there are other preferred approaches. Many gardeners rely on a four-step method called Integrated Pest Management [IPM]:

1. Identify the organism causing the problem [see Pest and Disease Solutions, pg. 69]. If you're unsure, bag the critter or affected foliage and take it to a nursery or a local extension office for an identification.

2. Monitor the damage. How severe is it? Is it getting better or worse? Sometimes letting nature take its course results in a natural control taking over: a good guy comes along to eat the bad guy.

3. Set expectation for levels of tolerable damage. Are your flowers being groomed for your sister's wedding or simply to provide spots of color in the garden?

4. Take action, beginning with the lowest-impact treatment [see Pest and Disease Solutions, pg. 69]. Use chemical controls sparingly, since they can kill beneficial insects, too, and cause an increase in pest populations. Try the following in turn: hand picking; biological controls; soap solutions; insecticidal soaps; naturally occurring pesticides such as rotenone and pyrethrin; synthetic pesticides.

(Top) Mosaic virus is an incurable, fatal plant disease. Plants with viral disease should be removed and discarded in household waste to prevent spread of the disease.

(Center) Most plant diseases are caused by fungus and are easily remedied.

(Bottom) Pests, such as spider mites, require prompt control.

APPLYING INSECTICIDAL SOAP

Insecticidal soap kills soft-bodied insects on contact with little impact to humans, the environment, or unsprayed creatures. It controls aphids, leafhoppers, mealybugs, mites, scale crawlers, and whiteflies. Find the listing for your pest on its label before application. Soaps are most effective when wet and become ineffective when dry. Gather together protective clothing, a measure, the soap, and a sprayer. Spray on a day with still air with temperatures less than 85°F (29°C), and follow these steps:

1 Always don protective gloves, goggles, and garments whenever you apply garden chemicals. Read and follow the package instructions exactly. Check for names of plants that can be damaged by insecticidal soap. Dilute the product with water, if appropriate, measuring carefully.

Warning

Restrict access by children and pets to treated areas until any health hazard has abated.

2 Apply soap spray directly to insect pests. Wet the flowers, leaves, stems, and especially the undersides of leaves where insects may hide. Avoid spraying uninfested areas. Let dry; repeat the application as needed.

3 Always dispose of empty containers and unused spray properly. Thoroughly wash spray implements, gloves, and utensils.

APPLYING BOTANICAL PESTICIDE SPRAYS

Warning
Restrict access by children and pets to treated areas until any health hazard has abated.

W hen your plants have an infestation that has resisted other controls, consider using sprays containing pyrethrin, a naturally occurring compound derived from chrysanthemum flowers. Identify the pest and check the package label for effectiveness on it before using any control product. Spray well-watered plants, in early morning, when air is still, and temperatures won't rise above 85°F (30°C). Be cautious when spraying new growth, seedlings, buds, and blossoms. Remember, keep pyrethrin away from ponds and streams. Products are available as ready-to-use and concentrate liquids, and in powder forms that must be diluted with water before application from a spray bottle. Follow these steps:

2 Choose a spray specific to your pest. Wear protective clothing, gloves, goggles, and a respirator whenever you apply garden chemical sprays.

1 Inspect your perennial plants regularly, especially checking the undersides of leaves where insects hide. Many pests are easily identified, such as the aphids pictured above. For help on less common insects, ask staff at your garden store or nursery, or call your local USDA or Agriculture Canada extension office.

3 Read and follow exactly all package label instructions for mixing, application, cleanup, and disposal.

4 Spray the insects themselves, avoiding spray of uninfested areas. Pyrethrin must contact the pests to be effective.

5 Allow the plant to thoroughly dry. Within 24 hours, all signs of the infestation should have abated. Inspect the plants again in 48 hours to discover any recurrences.

PEST AND DISEASE SOLUTIONS

Symptom	Cause	Remedies
Curled, twisted, sticky leaves; stunted or deformed blooms	Aphids; look for clusters of 1/16-in. (1.6-mm) green, yellow, or gray round insects	Spray with water from a hose; spray with solution of 2–3 T (30–44 ml) dishwashing liquid per gallon (4 l) of water; spray with insecticidal soap
Holes chewed in leaves and flowers; no slime trails	Beetles: Japanese beetles, root weevils, rose chafers	Hand pick; spray insects with pyrethrin or rotenone. Control in larval stage with parasitic nematodes (for weevils, chafers), *Bacillus thuringiensis* (BT), or milky spore disease (for Japanese beetles)
Leaves turn yellow, drop off; minute white webs on undersides	Spider mites; shake branch over white paper, and look for moving specks	Spray repeatedly with water to rinse off dustlike pests; spray with insecticidal soap; avoid use of sprays that kill natural predators
Yellow, stunted leaves; sticky plant; shaking plant provokes a cloud of white flying insects	Whiteflies; look for tiny, white, mothlike insects	Catch with sticky traps; spray water on undersides of leaves; spray insecticidal soap on tops and undersides of leaves; avoid sprays that kill natural predators including stingless parasitic wasps
Stunted plants; white cottony clusters in leaf axils	Mealybugs	Dab or spray with diluted rubbing alcohol; spray with insecticidal soap; spray with horticultural oil
White- or brown-speckled leaves; may be gummy or deformed	Thrips	Spray with water; release ladybugs; spray with insecticidal soap
White trails inside leaves	Leaf miners	Difficult to control but rarely harmful to plant; remove and destroy all affected leaves
Mottled white leaves; edges brown or yellow	Leafhoppers; small, green wedge-shaped insects	Spray with insecticidal soap; many natural enemies will quickly control infestation
Chewed leaves; silvery slime trails	Slugs and snails	Hand pick after dark; use copper foil barriers around beds or containers; use nontoxic baits of iron phosphate; use bait gel
Chewed blossoms	Earwigs	Set out traps of rolled newspaper or low-profile cans filled with 1/2 in. (13 mm) of vegetable oil; collect and destroy
Light powdery dusting of gray or white on leaves, flowers; deformed new growth	Powdery mildew	Spray affected parts with solution of 1 T (15 ml) baking soda and 3 T (44 ml) horticultural oil to 1 gallon (4 l) water; spray with sulfur fungicide
Flowers collapse under heavy fuzz of gray or brown fungal spores	Botrytis rot, also known as gray mold	Remove affected blossoms, foliage, or entire plant; space plants for more air circulation; reduce nitrogen fertilizer

PRUNING

Timely passes with pruning shears during the year help your plants produce more and larger blossoms. Prune regularly throughout the garden season to promote healthy growth, keep your garden tidy, and reduce the likelihood of pest infestation. Use sharp, clean shears and pruning tools; they'll reduce the effort and avoid damaging your plants.

In spring, as stems of garden phlox and other dense-foliage perennials sprout, cut off and remove one-third of the stalks at the ground, keeping the thickest ones. This thinning encourages the plant to put growth energy into bigger flowers. For late blooming plants such as asters and chrysanthemums, cut back stems by removing the top third of their stems when they reach 9–12 inches (23–30 cm) long. This promotes compact, dense growth, with many stems and more flowers.

Start deadheading in late spring as the first flowers fade—remove spent flowers by pinching or cutting, then repeat throughout the blooming cycle [see opposite]. Deadheading keeps the garden tidy and stimulates many perennials to produce new blooms. Deadhead cranesbill, sages, tickseeds, and yarrow for continuing blooms.

Pruning implements (clockwise from top left) include serrated flower shears, anvil hand pruner, bypass hand pruner, lopping shears, and folding pruning saw.

(Bottom) Removing dead flowers before they go to seed will prompt many perennial species to produce new buds and blooms. This process is called deadheading and usually is done with a pruning tool or by picking flowers with your fingers.

When your garden's purpose is to attract birds, skip deadheading. Seed heads of purple coneflower and perennial sunflowers develop into feeding stations that birds love. Plants such as eulalia grass and ornamental onion dry into pale or rusty tones that provide birds shelter and make handsome patterns against the snow all winter.

Other exceptions to deadheading flowers are those that self-sow. If you want your perennials to propagate themselves, leave some blooms to dry out and go to seed.

As the blooming season ends, do a general garden cleanup. Cut off yellowing foliage and remove spent flower stems. If foliage appears insect and disease free, leave it on the ground to over-winter as a mulch or compost it. The heat of composting will kill most disease and pest spores and eggs.

PROMOTING CONTINUAL BLOOMS

Deadheading—cutting off faded flowers—keeps your garden neat and fresh, lessens the likelihood of pests and disease, and promotes repeated blooming. Deadhead weekly from late spring through autumn using sharp hand pruners designed for smaller plants and cordless hand shears for larger perennials. Keep a pair of lightweight florist shears and a basket by the door for quick passes through smaller plants on summer evenings. To enjoy a full season of flowers, follow these steps:

1 Use hand shears to cut stemmed plants to a leaf just below faded flowers. New sprouts will emerge on the stalk. For species that resprout from the soil, cut the old stalk at the ground once new sprouts emerge.

2 Use a hedge trimmer to closely crop floppy plants such as lavender and catnip. Keeping plants full and compact prompts rebloom in long-season gardens.

3 Use a long-necked weeding fork to rid your beds of dry foliage from any spent plants.

PROPAGATING PERENNIALS

It's easy to multiply your perennial plants to transplant elsewhere in your garden or swap with friends. The following pages feature four ways to propagate perennials. The first three reproduce exact copies of your original host plant. The methods are:

Division: A foolproof method for creating multiple plants quickly, division involves digging up the host plant, carefully separating the most vigorous new buds or root divisions, and replanting them in amended soil. It works with plants that grow in clumping habits such as daylilies, grasses, coralbells, phlox, and delphiniums. Some fast-growing plants including Shasta daisies require division every few years to keep blooming and grow vigorously.

Cuttings: Most plants that have stems or branches with leaves can be propagated by taking cuttings. Cutting involves pruning a vigorous stem, dipping it in rooting hormone, and placing it in moistened rooting medium to sprout roots. It works for many perennials including chrysanthemum, delphinium, pinks, and sage. While this method is often less successful than division and takes longer to produce plants, it avoids digging or disturbing the host plant.

Layering: Burying a healthy stem so that it produces roots, then pruning the rooted stem, which becomes the new plant, is called layering. More commonly used for shrubs, flowering perennials that have flexible branches with leaves on them can be propagated through layering. While it can take longer than division or cuttings, layering avoids disturbing the host plant.

Seeds: Some perennials resist vegetative propagation; examples are balloon flowers, bleeding-heart, false indigo, monkshood, and peony. To reproduce these plants, collect and sow their seeds.

A potting bench is a convenient place to propagate perennials. Grow new plants from your favorites that have become crowded and require division, take cuttings, or plant seeds you have collected from spent flowers.

ROOT DIVISION

Divide plants that grow in thickets such as phlox, those that make fans of foliage including bearded iris, and those that produce low tufts of leaves including coralbells and thrift. Each spring, divide plants that bloom in late summer or autumn to ensure a long growing season; divide other plants after they bloom. Gather a shovel, two hand or spading forks, and a sharp knife. Water plants 24–48 hours before performing division, work on a cool, overcast day to keep roots moist, and follow these steps:

1 For fibrous-rooted plants, carefully dig up and shake soil off roots. Using two hand forks, pull the plant apart into sections bearing complete roots, crown, and leaves. Discard any incomplete or withered sections. Replant sections into amended soil, placing them at same depth at which they were growing. Water to settle the soil with half-strength liquid fertilizer.

2 For large plants with thick, heavy roots, use two spading forks to lever apart the roots and foliage, dividing the plant into two or more sections, each bearing roots, crowns, and foliage. Discard any incomplete or withered sections and pull off yellowing foliage. Replant divisions into amended soil, placing them at the same depth at which they were growing. Water with half-strength liquid fertilizer to settle the soil.

3 Divide rhizomatous plants after their flowers fade. Carefully dig up each rhizome. Remove shriveled rhizomes and roots plus any part that shows symptoms of pest or disease. Using a sharp knife, divide each rhizome into V-shaped pieces with two growing tips. Leave foliage intact. If desired, dust the root edges with fungicide powder to discourage disease. Replant the rhizome sections on the soil surface, with their roots underground. Water to settle the soil. Avoid using high-nitrogen fertilizer.

GROWING CUTTINGS

Take cuttings from plants that have branches bearing leaves. Gather together pruning shears, rooting hormone (available at nurseries and garden centers), stakes, clean pots or flats, and clean plastic bags. Fill the pots or flats with rooting medium. A rooting medium is one part peat moss to two parts perlite, moistened but not dripping wet. Take cuttings in spring or summer, water plants 24 hours before beginning, work on a cool, overcast day, and follow these steps:

2 Strip off leaves on the lower 2 in. (50 mm) of the cutting. Dip the cut end into rooting hormone.

1 Make cuttings 4–6 in. (10–15 cm) long from branch tips without flowers. Cut each clipping just below a node, which is the place on the stem where a leaf is attached. On the other end, cut just above a node, taking care to leave the leaf group attached to the cut piece.

3 Use a stick to make holes in rooting medium 2–3 in. (50–75 mm) deep and 2 in. (50 mm) apart. Put one cutting into each hole and firm around stem. Water and let drain.

5 After 2 weeks, check plants by gently tugging to see if any roots have sprouted. This process usually takes 2–4 weeks. When roots emerge, the offspring plant is ready for transplant.

4 Enclose the cutting container in a large plastic bag, positioning stakes to keep the bag off the foliage. Close the bag and set it in bright indirect light, where temperatures are between 65–75°F (18–24°C).

SOWING SEED AND LAYERING NEW PLANTS

Sowing Seed

1 Fill a clean bedding tray with sterile potting soil and place two seeds in each cell, at the depth recommended on the seed package.

Sow seed and layer existing plants to reproduce new planting stock for your garden. Grow plants from seed in spring a few weeks before the last frost is expected, always closely following the time of planting and depth recommendations on the seed package. When layering, choose stems with leaves; latent growth buds are found where the leaves meet the stem. Sow seed or layer when the plant is growing vigorously, and follow these steps:

2 Gently mist the soil surface with water from a spray bottle. Cover the flat and set it in bright, indirect light in a warm location.

3 When seedlings sprout, wait until two true leaves form above their seed leaves. Then transplant them into pots.

Layering

1 Select a stem without flower buds, bending it to the soil surface. Excavate a hole 2 in. (50 mm) deep. Make a small nick in the stem near its junction with a leaf axil. Dust the cut with rooting hormone.

2 Anchor the stem with a small U-shaped metal stake or with crossed wooden stakes. Cover the nicked stem and hole with soil. Water the soil thoroughly and regularly.

3 When roots emerge on the nicked stem, use pruning shears to cut the stem between the new roots and the host plant. The offspring plant is now ready for transplant.

COLD-CLIMATE CARE

Hardy perennials tolerate freezing well—as long as they stay frozen all winter long. It's the cycle of freezing and thawing that damages most perennials, rather than the sheer cold. Your task is to provide your perennials with an insulating mulch that allows your plants to gradually slow down in autumn and gradually start growing again in spring.

Winter care starts in midsummer. Summer is the last time for feeding plants with nitrogen, since nitrogen promotes growth of new leaves and shoots that will be hard hit by frost. In autumn, before the first frost, apply a new layer of organic mulch, 2–3 inches (50–75 mm) thick. It will insulate the soil so it retains late-season heat when roots are still active and help it stay cool in spring, so plants will remain dormant until the weather has warmed up.

After plants experience the first hard frost of the season, cut their stems to 8–10 inches (20–25 cm) long, adding these clippings to your compost pile. You may want to leave the interesting seed heads of decorative grasses and other plants, especially if the ground will be covered with snow.

In areas that experience combined cold temperatures and limited snow cover, give perennials a single-layer, protective covering of organic mulch such as weed-free straw, pine needles, chipped wood, or evergreen boughs. Cover the mulch with plastic net and weight it for wind protection. This covering protects the planting area from icy winds and keeps the ground frozen through cycles of freezing and thawing that otherwise might push unprotected plants out of the soil.

Most damage comes from autumn and spring frosts, when plants are growing. Be prepared to protect your perennial plants with such measures as fabric row covers, cotton bedsheets, or even cardboard boxes.

Even areas of mild climates experience the occasional frost. Warning signs to recognize are cold, cloudless nights with little wind and temperatures below 45°F (7°C) at 10 p.m. That's when you should lay on protection. An antitranspirant spray, available at nurseries and garden centers, will also provide a few degrees of frost insulation protection.

To care for badly frosted plants, wait until new growth sprouts—or well into spring—to prune damaged stems.

Winter's chilling temperatures are accompanied by soil freezing and thawing cycles that can disrupt and damage plant roots. A thick layer of mulch placed over and around the plants will insulate the soil. Keeping the soil frozen will protect the perennials' roots from harm.

WINTER PROTECTION

Where snow cover is scant, lay protective mulch on the bed as soon as the ground has frozen. Remove the mulch gradually in spring when danger of frost has passed. Use locally available products. Salt hay is available in the East, along with many other suitable mulches. Choose weed-free straw to avoid sprouts in spring. If gales are likely to blow across your garden, stake the protective mulch in place. Follow these steps:

1 Spread a layer of salt hay, weed-free straw, or pine needles 4 in. (10 cm) thick across the planting area. Place a second layer at right angles to the first.

2 For additional protection, add two layers of evergreen branches such as those cut from holiday decorations, needle side down. Alternate branches at right angles.

4 Protect the trunks of half-hardy deciduous shrubs with a layer of hay, then wrap them with weed barrier fabric or burlap secured with tied twine.

3 To secure from wind, cover with metal poultry netting or plastic bird netting, fastened to the ground with stakes or wire staples.

Choosing plants that thrive where you want them to bloom is key to growing a successful perennial garden. Selecting perennial plants you relish viewing is key to enjoying your yard year after year.

All the wonderful plants featured on the following pages are perennials as defined by horticulturists: plants with fibrous roots that grow and bloom for more than two years. Some are tender in cold climates, where they usually are treated as annuals.

Use this colorful encyclopedia as a visual identification guide. When you observe a plant you like in a private or public garden near your home, compare it to the 105 photographs found here to identify its planting needs and determine how you can use it in your garden design. Even when certain of the plant you want, use this encyclopedia to confirm information about it before going to your nursery or garden center. Common names vary regionally—compare the common and scientific names to be sure the plant you acquire is really the one you want.

Use it as a design tool. As you view the pictures and read the plant descriptions, check the foliage colors and textures, bloom colors and seasons, and other plant features. Then consider how you best can arrange plant massings to establish your chosen landscape style, make pleasing color combinations, and create vivid seasonal shows.

Use it as a written guide to plants that will succeed in your garden. Check for plants native or well adapted to your site conditions—the soil, sun, wind, and other climate factors —prevalent in your yard and your USDA plant hardiness zone [see USDA Plant hardiness Around the World, pg. 115]. Notice the necessary care level, and then consider your available time and interest in caring for the plants.

> **Photographs and vivid descriptions help you design your garden and make informed plant selections**

Encyclopedia of Flowering Perennials

Flowering perennials of every size, shape, bloom color, and description are available to fill your garden with their grace and beauty. Choose your plants from those on the pages that follow, picking those best suited to your garden, climate, and plant hardiness zone.

Common name: Anemone, Japanese; Windflower
Scientific name: *Anemone* × *hybrida*
Description: Open clusters of flowers 2–3 in. (50–75 mm) wide with yellow centers. Large, graceful, maplelike, light to deep green, leaves. Plants grow to 5 ft. (1.5 m) tall, 18 in. (45 cm) wide.
Bloom color/season: White, shades of pink. Late summer–autumn.
Plant hardiness: Zones 4–8.
Soil needs: Rich fertility, well-drained. Supplement with peat moss. Avoid soggy soil in winter. 7.0 pH.
Planting: Full sun to partial shade. 2 ft. (60 cm) apart. Plant in early spring or early autumn.
Care: Water regularly in dry weather. Mulch to protect from freezing. Propagate from seeds, division.
Features: Good choice for autumn color. Difficult to eradicate. Generally disease and pest resistant. Popular cultivars include 'Alba' with white flowers, 'Lesseri' with crimson flowers, and 'Rosea Superba' with pink flowers.

Common name: Aster, Hardy
Scientific name: *Aster* species
Description: Nearly 500 species of herbaceous perennials. Large clusters of daisylike flowers 2 in. (50 mm) wide with yellow centers. Medium-textured dark to dusty green leaves. Plants grow 9–72 in. (20–180 cm) tall. Mounding.
Bloom color/season: Blue, purple, red, pink, white. Late summer–autumn.
Plant hardiness: Zones 4–9.
Soil needs: Light, moist, well-drained. 5.5–7.5 pH.
Planting: Partial to full sun. 12–20 in. (30–50 cm) apart. Plant in spring.
Care: Easy. Water whenever soil dries. Fertilize lightly every few weeks. Stake and pinch tall species in late spring for compact growth. Divide in alternating years in early spring. Propagate from seeds, division, stem cuttings.
Features: Good choice for cut flowers. Aphid, mildew, root rot, and vascular-wilt susceptible. A popular North American native species is New England aster, *A. novae-angliae*.

Common name: Aster, Stokes'
Scientific name: *Stokesia laevis*
Description: Loose clusters of radiating flowers 3–4 in. (75–100 mm) wide with same-color fuzzy centers. Clumps of dark green leaves 2–8 in. (50–200 mm) long provide feathery texture. Plants grow 18–24 in. (45–60 cm) tall. Stately.
Bloom color/season: Blue, lavender, pink, white. July–October.
Plant hardiness: Zones 5–10.
Soil needs: Average fertility, well-drained. Avoid soggy soil in winter. 5.5–7.5 pH.
Planting: Full sun. 12–15 in. (30–38 cm) apart. Plant in early spring.
Care: Easy. Water moderately. Propagate from seeds, division, cuttings.
Features: Good choice for borders. Long blooming season. Generally disease resistant. A North American native.

Common name: Avens
Scientific name: *Geum* species
Description: Over 50 species of herbaceous perennials. Single or double roselike flowers. Irregular, toothed leaves. Dense foliage clumps. Plants grow 1–2 ft. (30–60 cm) tall, 12–18 in. (30–45 cm) wide. Small and ruffly.
Bloom color/season: Bright red, yellow, orange. May–July.
Plant hardiness: Zones 3–7.
Soil needs: Well-drained, rich in organic matter. 8.0 pH.
Planting: Full sun to partial shade. 12–18 in. (30–45 cm) apart. Plant in spring.
Care: Water abundantly during growing season. Propagate from seeds, division.
Features: Good choice for bright color accent at edge of shade garden, combining with plantain lily, woodland rock gardens. Best in regions of cool summers. Long lived. Downy mildew susceptible.

Common name: Baby's Breath
Scientific name: *Gypsophila paniculata*
Description: Clusters with hundreds of semi-double flowers $\frac{1}{16}$–$\frac{1}{8}$ in. (1.5–3 mm) wide in a single, multibranched panicle or branched group. Small, toothed leaves. Plants grow to 3 ft. (90 cm). Compact, delicate, feathery, and graceful.
Bloom color/season: Usually white, sometimes pink. Summer.
Plant hardiness: Zones 4–9.
Soil needs: Poor fertility, moist, well-drained. 7.0–9.0 pH.
Planting: Full sun. 24–30 in. (60–75 cm) apart. Plant in early spring.
Care: Water moderately. Stake to maintain form. Place a wire basket over young plants. Propagate from seeds, divisions, root cuttings.
Features: Good choice for borders, cut flowers, drying, edgings in rose gardens, rock gardens. Florists commonly use *G. paniculata* and *G. elegans* in floral arrangements. Leafhopper susceptible.

Common name: Balloon Flower
Scientific name: *Platycodon grandiflorus*
Description: Open, single, five-pointed star-shaped flowers 2–3 in. (50–75 mm) wide on slender stalks at the ends of upright stems. Dense, oval leaves, 1–3 in. (25–75 mm) long, medium green above and bluish beneath. Plants grow 18–30 in. (45–75 cm) tall.
Bloom color/season: Deep to pale blue, pink, white. Late June–September.
Plant hardiness: Zones 3–9.
Soil needs: Sandy or loam, well-drained. 7.0–7.5 pH.
Planting: Full sun to partial shade. 12–18 in. (30–45 cm) apart. Plant in spring.
Care: Easy. Water moderately. Requires no special attention. Propagate from seeds, divisions. Slow to emerge, mark location if started from seed.
Features: Good choice for borders, color-themed gardens. Long lived. Gopher, nematode, southern blight susceptible.

Common name: Beard-tongue
Scientific name: *Penstemon* species
Description: About 250 species of herbaceous and shrub perennials. Tubular blossoms flare at mouth. Narrow, pointed, glossy leaves, 2–4 in. (50–100 mm) long. Bushy plants with upright stems. Plants grow 2–3 ft. (60–90 cm) tall.
Bloom color/season: Rose, pink, red, purple, white; some bicolor with white, delicately spotted throat. Spring–summer.
Plant hardiness: Zones 3–10.
Soil needs: Average fertility, sandy, well-drained. Avoid soggy conditions in winter, hot dry locations in summer. 5.5–6.5 pH.
Planting: Full sun or partial shade. 12–18 in. (30–45 cm) apart. Plant in spring.
Care: Water moderately. Deadhead for repeat blooming. Propagate from seeds, division, cuttings.
Features: Good choice for color, borders. Attracts butterflies and hummingbirds. Nearly all are North American natives.

Common name: Bee Balm; Bergamot; Oswego Tea; Red Balm
Scientific name: *Monarda didyma*
Description: Single or double whorls of fluffy, dense, tubular, double-lipped irregular flowers 2 in. (50 mm) long. Branching stems of oval, pointed, downy on under surface, toothed leaves, 3–6 in. (75–150 mm) long. Plants grow to 4 ft. (1.2 m) tall. Bushy and erect.
Bloom color/season: Scarlet, pink, white. June–August.
Plant hardiness: Zones 4–9.
Soil needs: Average fertility, moist, rich in organic matter. 6.5–7.0 pH.
Planting: Partial shade. 2 ft. (60 cm) apart. Plant in spring.
Care: Easy. Water abundantly. Avoid fertilizer. Propagate from seeds, root divisions in spring.
Features: Good choice to mass in borders, natural gardens. Attracts butterflies, hummingbirds, bees. Used in some oils and perfumes to mask chemical odors. Leaves make mintlike tea. Powdery mildew, rust susceptible.

Common name: Begonia
Scientific name: *Begonia* × *tuberhybrida* hybrids
Description: A group of cultivars derived from several species. Double or triple flowers up to 6 in. (15 cm) wide. Pointed, glossy, bright to dark green leaves 6 in. (15 cm) long. Plants grow 12–18 in. (30–45 cm) tall. Some are fragrant. Erect, bushy, or trailing.
Bloom color/season: White, pink, red, yellow, orange. Summer.
Plant hardiness: Cold-hardy. Zones 6–11. Lift in autumn in other zones or treat as annual.
Soil needs: Rich fertility, moist, well-drained. 6.5 pH.
Planting: Shade with bright light. 10–18 in. (25–45 cm) apart. Plant in summer.
Care: Water regularly. Fertilize sparingly. Avoid overcrowding. Deadhead to prolong blooming. Store lifted tubers in dry place. Propagate from seeds, division of tubers, leaf cuttings.
Features: Good choice for containers, hanging containers in shady borders.

Common name: Bellflower, Willow; Peach-bells
Scientific name: *Campanula persicifolia*
Description: Dainty, loose sprays of cupped single or double flowers 1½ in. (38 mm) wide. Narrow leaves 4–8 in. (10–20 cm) long. Plants grow 2–3 ft. (60–90 cm) tall. Low, slender, leafy.
Bloom color/season: Blue, purple, white. Spring–summer.
Plant hardiness: Zones 3–10.
Soil needs: Average fertility, well-drained. Add compost or peat moss at planting time. 7.0 pH.
Planting: Full sun to partial shade. 12–18 in. (30–45 cm) apart.
Care: Water regularly. Divide crowded clumps in early spring or autumn. Propagate from seeds, division, cuttings.
Features: Good choice for borders, cut flowers, rock gardens. Evergreen in warmer climates. Aster yellows susceptible.

Common name: Bergenia
Scientific name: *Bergenia cordifolia*
Description: Clusters of showy flowers ¾ in. (19 mm) wide. Glossy, wavy-edged, hairy, mostly evergreen leaves 6–10 in. (15–25 cm) wide. Thick, creeping rootstocks form gradually expanding clumps. Plants grow 18 in. (45 cm) tall.
Bloom color/season: Rose-colored, dark pink, white. Early spring.
Plant hardiness: Zones 3–8.
Soil needs: Average to rich fertility, well-drained. 6.0–7.5 pH.
Planting: Partial shade. 1 ft. (30 cm) apart. Plant in spring.
Care: Easy. Very cold tolerant. Water regularly. Propagate from seeds, divide and replant crowded or leggy plantings in late winter or early spring. Fertilize if you plan to divide frequently.
Features: Good choice for ground covers. Nematode susceptible.

Common name: Blanket Flower
Scientific name: *Gaillardia* × *grandiflora*
Description: Single or semi-double flowers 3–4 in. (75–100 mm) wide with dark- to red-purple, yellow, or brown centers. Alternate, lance-shaped, medium- to rough-textured, hairy, dark gray green leaves. Plants grow 2–3 ft. (60–90 cm) tall, 12–18 in. (30–45 cm) wide. Bushy.
Bloom color/season: Yellow, deep red, gold tipped in yellow. Early summer–autumn.
Plant hardiness: Zones 3–8.
Soil needs: Average to poor fertility, sandy or loam, well-drained to dry. Avoid retentive clay soils. 6.0–7.5 pH.
Planting: Full sun. 10–15 in. (25–38 cm) apart. Start in early spring.
Care: Easy. Water moderately; avoid overwatering. Spreads by rhizomes. Stake taller plants. Prune roots in summer. Divide crowded or patchy clumps annually in spring. Propagate from seeds, division.
Features: Good choice for cut flowers. Aphid, leaf spot, powdery mildew susceptible.

Common name: Blazing Star; Button Snakeroot; Gay-feather
Scientific name: *Liatris* species
Description: About 40 species of perennials. Small bright flowers rise from foxtail-like leafy spike. Alternate, foxtail-like, very narrow, lance-shaped leaves to 16 in. (40 cm) long cover stems. Plants grow 2–5 ft. (60–150 cm) tall, 12–18 in. (30–45 cm) wide. Erect.
Bloom color/season: Lilac to deep purple, red, white. Late summer–autumn.
Plant hardiness: Zones 4–9.
Soil needs: Poor fertility, sandy, well-drained to dry. 5.5–7.5 pH.
Planting: Full sun. 12–15 in. (30–38 cm) apart. Plant in spring.
Care: Easy. Water moderately. Plants grow tall in rich soil and require staking. Most species grow from corms. Propagate from seeds, division.
Features: Good choice for cut flowers, natural gardens, vertical accent. Rust, southern root-knot nematode susceptible. North American native.

Common name: Bleeding-heart; Dutchman's Breeches
Scientific name: *Dicentra* species
Description: About 19 species of perennials. Puffy, heart-shaped, tipped flowers droop nearly horizontally in sprays. Feathery, dense, compound, heart-shaped, medium grayish green foliage. Plants grow 12–30 in. (30–75 cm) tall, 3 ft. (90 cm) wide. Arching.
Bloom color/season: Pink, red, purple, white. April–June.
Plant hardiness: Zones 3–9.
Soil needs: Average fertility, well-drained, rich in organic matter. Dies out in wet soils. 7.0–8.0 pH.
Planting: Filtered sun to partial shade. Avoid drying winds. 3 ft. (90 cm) apart. Plant in early spring.
Care: Water abundantly, feed regularly, cut back when dormancy begins. Keep roots cool and moist. Divide crowns or roots in early spring. Propagate from seeds, division of crowns or roots.
Features: Good choice for grouping with spreading plants. Stem rot, vascular wilt susceptible.

Common name: Bluebells; Cowslip; or Lungwort
Scientific name: *Mertensia* species
Description: About 40 species of perennials. Nodding clusters of drooping, bell-shaped flowers 1 in. (25 mm) long. Alternate, oval, blue green leaves 8 in. (20 cm) long in basal rosettes. Plants grow 1–3 ft. (30–90 cm) tall, 1 ft. (30 cm) wide. Erect, gracefully relaxed.
Bloom color/season: Some have pink buds and new flowers that change to lavender or blue. Spring–early summer.
Plant hardiness: Zones 3–9.
Soil needs: Rich fertility, moist, rich in organic matter. 7.0 pH.
Planting: Full sun to partial shade. 8–12 in. (20–30 cm) apart. Plant from nursery containers in early spring or seeds in autumn.
Care: Easy. Keep soil moist. Propagate from seeds, division.
Features: Good choice for natural gardens. Foliage disappears by July. Some are fungal disease susceptible.

Common name: Bluestar
Scientific name: *Amsonia Tabernaemontana*
Description: Tiny star clusters of drumsticklike flowers ¾ in. (19 mm) long with light blue centers. Willowlike, glossy, bright green leaves 9 in. (23 cm) long, turn yellow in autumn. Plants grow to 3 ft. (90 cm) tall, 18–24 in. (45–60 cm) wide. Delicate, bushy semi-erect.
Bloom color/season: Steel blue. May–June.
Plant hardiness: Zones 3–9.
Soil needs: Average to moderately rich fertility, well-drained. Avoid soggy soil. 7.0 pH.
Planting: Full sun to partial shade. 6–9 in. (15–23 cm) apart. Plant in autumn or spring.
Care: Water regularly to moderately. Fertilize regularly. Propagate from seeds or division in early spring or stem cuttings in summer.
Features: Good choice for borders, cut flowers. Grows slowly. Long lived.

Common name: Bugbane; Rattletop
Scientific name: *Cimicifuga* species
Description: About 15 species of herbaceous perennials. Dense small, bristly flowers cover upper 2 ft. (60 cm) of slender, wandlike spikes. Compound, coarsely fernlike, glossy, dark green leaves. Plants grow 30–96 in. (75–240 cm) tall, 2 ft. (60 cm) wide. Tall, slender.
Bloom color/season: White. June–September.
Plant hardiness: Zones 3–9.
Soil needs: Rich fertility, moist, rich in organic matter. 6.0 pH.
Planting: Filtered sun to partial shade. 2 ft. (60 cm) apart. Plant in early spring.
Care: Easy. Water regularly. Stake and pinch for beauty and growth. Propagate from seeds, division in early spring or autumn.
Features: Good choice for back of beds. Sweet fragrance.

Common name: Bugloss; Alkanet
Scientific name: *Anchusa* species
Description: About 35 species of annuals and perennials. Drooping spikes of large, loose clusters of vivid, tube-shaped flowers ½ in. (13 mm) wide. Alternate, coarse, dark green leaves, 3–4 in. (75–100 mm) long. Plants grow 3–5 ft. (90–150 cm) tall. Upright and spreading.
Bloom color/season: Bright blues, violet, white. May–July.
Plant hardiness: Zones 3–8.
Soil needs: Average to poor fertility, loam, moist, well-drained. 6.0–7.5 pH.
Planting: Full sun to partial shade, out of wind. 18–30 in. (45–75 cm) apart. Plant in spring.
Care: Easy. Water moderately. Stake tall varieties. Avoid fertilizer. Propagate from seeds, root cuttings.
Features: Good choice for backgrounds, borders, cut flowers, fences. Crown rot, leafhopper susceptible.

Common name: Bugloss, Siberian; Brunnera
Scientific name: *Brunnera macrophylla*
Description: Light, delicate clusters of showy flowers ¼ in. (6 mm) wide on wiry, slightly hairy stems. Alternate heart-shaped, variegated leaves 4 in. (10 cm) wide, 6–8 in. (15–20 cm) long. Plant grows 18–24 in. (45–60 cm) tall, 12–18 in. (30–45 cm) wide. Bushy, clean, lush appearance.
Bloom color/season: Blue. Spring–summer.
Plant hardiness: Zones 3–10.
Soil needs: Rich fertility, moist, rich in organic matter. 7.0 pH.
Planting: Partial shade. 1 ft. (30 cm) apart. Plant in autumn.
Care: Easy. Water average to moderately. Propagate from seeds, division, root cuttings in winter.
Features: Good choice for border edges, filler, small-scale ground cover, under taller shrubs. Disease and pest resistant.

Common name: Burning Bush; Gas Plant; Fraxinella
Scientific name: *Dictamnus albus*
Description: Showy, loose spikes of flowers 1 in. (25 mm) long with prominent pistils. Alternate, dense, oval, glossy, dotted leaves 3 in. (75 mm) long. Plants grow 30–36 in. (75–90 cm) tall, 3–6 ft. (90–180 cm) wide. Shrublike and bushy, with interesting foliage textures.
Bloom color/season: Purple to rosy pink, white. Late spring–summer.
Plant hardiness: Zones 3–8.
Soil needs: Average to rich fertility, well-drained, rich in organic matter. Avoid soggy soils. 7.0 pH.
Planting: Full sun to partial shade. 3 ft. (90 cm) apart. Plant in spring.
Care: Little care once established. Water moderately. Fertilize occasionally. Propagate from seeds, division.
Features: Good choice for back of borders. Long lived. Citrus scented. Oil in immature seed pods is lightly flammable.

Common name: Buttercup
Scientific name: *Ranunculus* species
Description: About 250 species of annuals, biennials, and perennials. Single and some double flowers. Alternate, lobed or divided leaves. Head of small, dry fruit is ornamental.
Bloom color/season: Usually bright yellow; also orange, red, pink, white. Spring–summer.
Plant hardiness: Zones 3–6.
Soil needs: Average fertility, moist, well-drained. 7.0 pH.
Planting: Partial to full shade. Plant in spring.
Care: Easy. Water moderately. The florists' species, *R. asiaticus*, is a tuberous root that must be stored in cold-winter climates. Garden species are more hardy. Propagate from seeds, division in spring.
Features: Good choice for ground cover in woodland gardens. Some well-adapted to water garden shorelines.

Common name: Candytuft
Scientific name: *Iberis sempervirens*
Description: Flat clusters of showy flowers with 4 small petals. Narrow, dense, glossy, dark green leaves 1½ in. (38 mm) long. Plants grow 8–12 in. (20–30 cm) tall, 16–36 in. (40–90 cm) wide. Compact, low, wide.
Bloom color/season: White. Spring.
Plant hardiness: Zones 3–10.
Soil needs: Rich fertility, well-drained. 6.0–7.0 pH.
Planting: Full sun to slight shade. 6–12 in. (15–30 cm) apart. Plant in spring.
Care: Very easy. Water to keep ground moist. Deadhead for repeat blooming, to keep plants compact. Propagate from seeds, division, cuttings.
Features: Good choice for accents, borders, containers, edging, evening gardens. Evergreen foliage looks good all year. Heirloom plant. Disease resistant, snails eat blossoms.

Common name: Catmint
Scientific name: *Nepeta* species
Description: About 250 species of annuals and perennials. Clusters of flowers ¼ in. (6 mm) long on tall spikes. Opposite, oval or triangular grayish leaves to 2 in. (50 mm) long. Plants grow 1–2 ft. (30–60 cm) tall. Billowy, dense.
Bloom color/season: Whitish to pale purple with pale purple spots. Spring–summer.
Plant hardiness: Zones 3–7.
Soil needs: Sandy, moist. 7.0 pH.
Planting: Full sun. 6 in. (15 cm) apart. Plant in early spring.
Care: Very easy. Water regularly but moderately. Cut old growth in early spring. Propagate from seeds, division.
Features: Good choice for beds, containers, ground cover. Fragrant. Catnip, *N. cataria*, is especially attractive to felines. Roots spread rapidly. Widespread weed in northern U.S. and southern Canada. Leafhopper susceptible.

Common name: Chinese-lantern
Scientific name: *Physalis Alkekengi* or *Abutilon hybridum* (shown)
Description: Two superficially similar plants of different genera are named Chinese lantern. Nodding flowers ¼ in. (6 mm) wide with whitish centers. Alternate, oval, hairy leaves to 3½ in. (90 mm) long. Brilliant, lantern-shaped husk 2 in. (50 mm) long holds, in *P. alkekengi*, small, edible, cherrylike fruit and, in *A. hybridum*, colorful stamens. Plants grow 2 ft. (60 cm) tall.
Bloom color/season: White, bright red fruit husks. Summer.
Plant hardiness: *P. alkekengi* zones 2–10; *A. hybridum* zone 9.
Soil needs: Well-drained. 7.0 pH.
Planting: Full sun to partial shade. Plant in early spring.
Care: Water moderately. Propagate from seeds, division.
Features: Grown for ornamental fruit husks used in dried arrangements. Avoid use in mixed plantings as they are invasive.

> **Warning**
>
> *A. hybridum* may cause stomach upset if ingested or skin irritation in sensitive individuals.

Common name: Chrysanthemum

Scientific name: *Chrysanthemum* species

Description: Nearly 200 species of annuals and perennials. Mostly double, also single or clusters of profuse flowers 1–6 in. (25–150 mm) wide. Usually dense, deep green leaves. Plants grow 1–5 ft. (30–150 cm) tall, 18–24 in. (45–60 cm) wide. Bushy and compact to tall and upright, depending on species and variety.

Bloom color/season: Most colors except blue. August–November.

Plant hardiness: Zones 6–10.

Soil needs: Rich fertility, well-drained. 6.0–7.0 pH.

Planting: Full sun to partial shade. 18 in. (45 cm) apart. Plant in spring.

Care: Water regularly, especially during drought. Mulch after ground freezes. Fertilize. Pinch tall varieties for larger flowers. Cut to ground level after freeze. Propagate from seeds, division annually as growth begins, cuttings.

Features: Good choice for borders, containers, cut flowers. Often fragrant. Aphid susceptible.

Common name: Clematis

Scientific name: *Clematis* species

Description: Over 200 species of vines and herbs. Clusters of flat flowers 1–2 in. (25–50 mm) wide. Opposite, usually compound, broadly oval leaves 3–5 in. (75–125 mm) long. Plants grow 2–4 ft. (60–120 cm) tall. Bushy.

Bloom color/season: Brilliant blue, white. Summer.

Plant hardiness: Zones 4–9.

Soil needs: Rich fertility, well-aerated, moist, well-drained. Add some lime if soil is low in calcium. 6.5–7.5 pH.

Planting: Full sun to partial shade. 1 ft. (30 cm) apart.

Care: Easy. Water regularly. Mulch or shade roots with foliage of other plants. Propagate from seeds, division in early spring, cuttings in spring, layering. Prune wood to 1 ft. (30 cm) or less. Stake. Grow hybrids on trellises or posts.

Features: Good choice for accents to shrubs, borders. Fragrant. Of the 22 species only 3 are non-vining perennials. Aphid, fungus, nematode susceptible.

Common name: Columbine

Scientific name: *Aquilegia* species

Description: About 70 species of hardy perennials. Dainty, cup-and-saucer shape, showy flowers 1½–4 in. (38–100 mm) wide, up to 6 in. (15 cm) long. Fine-textured, light silvery green leaves. Plants grow 18–36 in. (45–90 cm) tall, 1–2 ft. (30–60 cm) wide. Delicate, airy, open, upright.

Bloom color/season: Mostly white, yellow, blue, bicolor. Early summer.

Plant hardiness: Zones 3–10.

Soil needs: Average to rich fertility, sandy or loam, very well-drained, rich in organic matter. 7.5 pH.

Planting: Full sun to partial shade. 1–2 ft. (30–60 cm) apart. Plant in midspring.

Care: Easy. Fertilize regularly and lightly. Propagate from seeds, division.

Features: Good choice for massing in borders, containers in shade, natural gardens. Attracts hummingbirds and bees. Aphid, powdery mildew, rust, wilt disease susceptible.

Common name: Coneflower
Scientific name: *Rudbeckia* species
Description: About 25 species of annuals, biennials, and perennials. Abundant flowers 3–4 in. (75–100 mm) wide with dark central cones. Alternate, broadly lance-shaped, hairy leaves. Plants grow 24–30 in. (60–75 cm) tall, 1–2 ft. (30–60 cm) wide. Erect, vase-shaped.
Bloom color/season: Deep yellow. Late summer–autumn.
Plant hardiness: Zones 3–9.
Soil needs: Almost any soil and location. Average to rich fertility, moist, well-drained. 7.0 pH.
Planting: Full sun to partial shade. 1–2 ft. (30–60 cm) apart. Plant in spring or autumn.
Care: Easy. Water moderately. Propagate from seeds, division, cuttings.
Features: Good choice for accents, cut flowers. Attracts butterflies. Aphid, downy mildew, rust, powdery mildew susceptible.

Common name: Coneflower, Purple
Scientific name: *Echinacea purpurea*
Description: Flat or drooping flowers 3–6 in. (75–150 mm) wide with dark conelike centers. Alternate, oval to narrow, rough-textured leaves 4–8 in. (10–20 cm) long. Plants grow 2–4 ft. (60–120 cm), rarely up to 6 ft. (1.8 m) tall, 2–5 ft. (60–150 cm) wide. Tall and upright.
Bloom color/season: Purple, red, pink, white. July–September.
Plant hardiness: Zones 3–10.
Soil needs: Rich fertility, sandy or clay, well-drained. Avoid soggy soil. 7.0 pH.
Planting: Full sun to partial shade. Can handle wind. 18–24 in. (45–60 cm) apart. Plant in spring.
Care: Easy. Water moderately. Fertilize lightly. Mulch. Propagate from seeds, division after about 4 years.
Features: Good choice for borders, cut flowers, natural gardens. Attracts butterflies. Downy and powdery mildew, Japanese beetle, mites, rust, southern blight susceptible.

Common name: Coralbells
Scientific name: *Heuchera sanguinea*
Description: Clusters 2–4 in. (50–100 mm) wide of tiny, bell-like flowers. Rounded to heart-shaped, hairy, dark green or silver mottled evergreen leaves. Plants grow 1–2 ft. (30–60 cm) tall, 12–18 in. (30–45 cm) wide. Airy and tall flower stems above low tufts of evergreen foliage.
Bloom color/season: Red, pink, white, chartreuse. Late May–autumn.
Plant hardiness: Zones 3–10.
Soil needs: Rich fertility, loam, moist, well-drained. 6.0–7.0 pH.
Planting: Full sun to partial shade. 9–15 in. (23–40 cm) apart.
Care: Easy. Water regularly, especially during drought. Cover loosely during winter. Propagate from seeds, division in early spring or autumn.
Features: Good choice for edging, rock gardens. Attracts hummingbirds. Mealy bug, nematode, root weevil, stem rot susceptible.

Common name: Cosmos, Black
Scientific name: *Cosmos atrosanguineus*
Description: Single, conspicuously colored, daisylike flowers 1 ½ in. (38 mm) wide with black centers on wiry stems. Opposite, bright green leaves divided into 5–7 very fine threadlike segments. Plants grow 18–24 in. (45–60 cm) tall.
Bloom color/season: Dark brownish red. July–frost.
Plant hardiness: Zones 7–10.
Soil needs: Rich fertility, sandy, well-drained. 5.0–8.0 pH.
Planting: Full sun. 18 in. (45 cm) apart. Plant in early spring.
Care: Water regularly. Propagate from seeds in summer or autumn, cuttings of separate tuberous roots in spring before growth starts.
Features: Good choice for containers, front of late-blooming flower gardens. Provides excellent color contrast with white and yellow blooms including Shasta daisy and sunflowers, and blue false indigo. All can be started from seed in well-prepared soil. Striking chocolate color and scent. Aphid, red spider mite susceptible.

Common name: Cranesbill
Scientific name: *Geranium sanguineum*
Description: Single, 5-petal flowers 1–2 in. (25–50 mm) wide. Maple-like to finely cut, bright green leaves 2 in. (50 mm) long, turn bright red in autumn. Plants grow 6–18 in. (15–45 cm) tall, 2 ft. (60 cm) wide. Mounded, spreading.
Bloom color/season: Purple red to magenta, white. May–August.
Plant hardiness: Zones 3–10.
Soil needs: Average fertility, moist, well-drained. Avoid very wet and very dry soil. 6.0–8.0 pH.
Planting: Full sun to partial shade. 1 ft. (30 cm) apart. Plant in spring after hazard of frost has passed.
Care: Moderately easy. Water regularly. Avoid overfertilizing. Propagate from seeds, root division.
Features: Good choice for borders, filler. Ornamental dense foliage mat. Downy mildew, leaf spot, nematode susceptible.

Common name: Cupid's-dart
Scientific name: *Catananche caerulea*
Description: Numerous narrow, notched petals form flowers 2 in. (50 mm) wide with dark centers. Alternate, narrow, somewhat toothed, woolly, gray green leaves to 1 ft. (30 cm) long. Plants grow 18 in. (45 cm) tall, 1 ft. (30 cm) wide. Grasslike.
Bloom color/season: Blue, white. June–early autumn.
Plant hardiness: Zones 3–8.
Soil needs: Average fertility, dry, well-drained. Avoid winter moistness. 7.0 pH.
Planting: Full sun. 1 ft. (30 cm) apart. Plant after last frost.
Care: Water moderately. Fertilize lightly and infrequently. Propagate from seeds, divisions.
Features: Good choice for borders, cut or dried flowers. Rot susceptible.

Common name: Daisy, Shasta
Scientific name: *Chrysanthemum × superbum*
Description: Bold, friendly, multipetaled flowers 2–6 in. (50–150 mm) wide. Coarsely toothed, glossy, dark green leaves. Plants grow 2–3 ft. (60–90 cm) tall in thick clumps.
Bloom color/season: White petals with gold centers. June–frost.
Plant hardiness: Zones 4–10.
Soil needs: Rich fertility, well-drained. 7.0 pH.
Planting: Full sun to partial shade. 2 ft. (60 cm) apart. Plant in spring.
Care: Very easy. Water regularly. Stake taller stems or plant near shrubs or rocks for support. Propagate from seeds, division in spring.
Features: Good choice for casual cottage, classic borders, cut flowers, natural gardens. Long blooming. Cultivars offer double flowers, compact growth. Nematode susceptible.

Common name: Daisy, Transvaal
Scientific name: *Gerbera Jamesonii*
Description: Exotic single or double, daisylike flowers 2–5 in. (50–125 mm) wide with pale red centers. Oblong, lobed, very hairy above and woolly beneath, gray green leaves to 10 in. (25 cm) long. Plants grow to 18 in. (45 cm) tall.
Bloom color/season: Orange red; hybrid has many other colors. Summer–autumn.
Plant hardiness: Zones 8–11. Protect from frost; use containers in colder zones.
Soil needs: Rich fertility, moist, well-drained. 6.5 pH.
Planting: Full sun to partial shade. 6–12 in. (15–30 cm) apart. Plant in spring.
Care: Water deeply and let dry out between waterings. Protect in winter. Deadhead for longer flowering time. Propagate from seeds, division, cuttings.
Features: Good choice for accents, containers, cut flowers. Root rot, slug, snail susceptible.

Common name: Daylily
Scientific name: *Hemerocallis* species
Description: About 15 species of perennials. Single or double chalice- or lily-shaped flowers 1–10 in. (25–250 mm) wide, up to 50 buds per stalk. Grasslike, sword-shaped, bright green, some evergreen leaves 1–2 ft. (30–60 cm) long. Plants grow 1–7 ft. (30–210 cm) tall, 18–36 in. (45–90 cm) wide. Clumping.
Bloom color/season: Yellow, orange, reddish, purple, cream, pink, striped, and bicolor. Spring–summer. Each flower lasts 1 day.
Plant hardiness: Zones 3–10.
Soil needs: Average fertility, dry, well-drained, rich in organic matter. Avoid very rich soil. 7.0 pH.
Planting: Full sun to partial shade. 18–36 in. (45–90 cm) apart. Plant in spring or late summer.
Care: Very easy. Water moderately. Fertilize lightly in spring or early summer. Provide protection for evergreen types in winter. Propagate from seeds, division every 3–5 years.
Features: Good choice for difficult areas, dried flowers. Nematode susceptible.

Common name: Delphinium; Larkspur
Scientific name: *Delphinium* species
Description: More than 300 species of annuals, biennials, and perennials. Single and double, starlike flowers up to 3 in. (8 cm) wide with white, black, or gold centers on stalks. Large-lobed, fanlike, dark green leaves. Plants grow 1–8 ft. (30–240 cm) tall, 18–36 in. (45–90 cm) wide. Most tall, some low and fluffy.

Bloom color/season: Mostly blues, purples; occasionally pink, white, cream, bicolor. Summer.
Plant hardiness: Zones 3–10.
Soil needs: Rich fertility, moist, well-drained, rich in organic matter. Avoid clay soil. 7.0 pH.
Planting: Full sun to partial shade. 18–36 in. (45–90 cm) apart. Plant in spring.
Care: Easy. Soak soil around roots, especially during growth. Fertilize in early and late season. Mulch well after ground freezes. Protect from wind. Stake at 1 ft. (30 cm); tie blooms. Deadhead and feed mixed fertilizer for repeat blooming. Propagate from seeds, division, softwood cuttings.
Features: *D. elatum* is good choice for classic backgrounds, cut flowers. Needs air circulation. Attracts hummingbirds and butterflies. Fungal disease, aphid, slug, snail susceptible.

> **Warning**
>
> All parts of delphinium are toxic if ingested. Avoid planting in areas frequented by children and pets.

Common name: Dusty-miller
Scientific name: *Senecio cineraria*
Description: Multipetaled flowers ½ in. (13 mm) wide. Attractive, lacelike, blunt-lobed, wooly, silvery white leaves. Plants grow 2 ft. (60 cm) tall. Stiff, dense, and bushy.
Bloom color/season: Yellow. Late spring–early autumn.
Plant hardiness: Zones 3–10.
Soil needs: Rich fertility, loam, well-drained. 7.0 pH.
Planting: Full sun. 1 ft. (30 cm) apart. Set seedlings out after frost.
Care: Easy. Water moderately. Pinch back for bushiness. Propagate from seeds, divisions, stem or root cuttings.
Features: Good choice for containers, contrast of attractive light-colored foliage, cottage gardens, formal beds. Grown for foliage, flowers are inconsequential. Very susceptible to a variety of diseases and pests.

Common name: Flax
Scientific name: *Linum perenne*
Description: Circular flowers 1–1¾ in. (25–44 mm) wide on hairy stems. Alternate, narrow, short leaves. Plants grow 18–24 in. (45–60 cm) tall. Thin, fine textured, graceful.
Bloom color/season: Bright blue, white, yellow. Spring–summer.
Plant hardiness: Zones 4–10.
Soil needs: Sandy or loam, well-drained. 7.0 pH.
Planting: Full sun. 1 in. (25 mm) apart. Plant in spring or summer.
Care: Easy. Water moderately. Light winter mulch. Propagate from seeds, division, cuttings.
Features: Good choice for bed foregrounds, rock gardens.

Common name: Fleabane
Scientific name: *Erigeron* species
Description: Almost 200 species of mostly perennials. Single, semi-double, or clustered flowers 1½–2 in. (38–50 mm) wide with threadlike petals and yellow centers. Alternate, narrow, pointed leaves. Plants grow to 2 ft. (60 cm) tall. Bushy.
Bloom color/season: Soft purple, blue, yellow, pink, white; rarely orange or yellow. Summer.
Plant hardiness: Zones 3–10.
Soil needs: Poor to average fertility, sandy or loam, well-drained. 7.0 pH.
Planting: Full sun to partial shade. 18 in. (45 cm) apart. Plant in early to midspring.
Care: Easy. Water infrequently. Propagate from seeds, division, cuttings.
Features: Good choice for natural, rock gardens.

Common name: Foamflower
Scientific name: *Tiarella cordifolia*
Description: Spikes of small, drooping flowers. Triangular to heart-shaped, toothed, lobed, strongly veined, downy basal leaves. Plants grow 6–12 in. (15–30 cm) tall. Low, bushy.
Bloom color/season: White to reddish. April–July.
Plant hardiness: Zones 3–9.
Soil needs: Moist. 7.0 pH.
Planting: Partial to full shade. 12–18 in. (30–45 cm) apart. Plant in late summer after heat has moderated.
Care: Water regularly. Avoid excessive winter moisture. Propagate from seeds, division.
Features: Good choice for borders, ground cover, natural gardens. After blooms fade, attractive, brilliantly colored foliage in autumn.

Common name: Foxglove
Scientific name: *Digitalis* species
Description: About 19 species of perennials. Large, showy, drooping, bell-shaped flowers, 2 in. (50 mm) long. Often very long, hairy, gray green lower leaves. Plants grow 2–5 ft. (60–150 cm) tall, 18–24 in. (45–60 cm) wide. Tall and stately.

> **Warning**
>
> All parts of foxglove are fatally toxic if ingested. Avoid planting in areas frequented by children and pets.

Bloom color/season: Mostly yellowish marked with brown, pink; also purple, yellow, brownish, white center; sometimes spotted, streaked. Summer.
Plant hardiness: Zones 4–9.
Soil needs: Rich fertility, moist, well-drained. Supplement with leaf mold. 6.5–7.0 pH.
Planting: Filtered sun to partial shade. 15–18 in. (40–45 cm) apart. Plant in early spring.
Care: Easy. Water regularly. Propagate from seeds, division in early spring
Features: Good choice for accents in woodland gardens. Leaf spot, Japanese beetle susceptible.

Common name: Gazania

Scientific name: *Gazania* species

Description: About 16 species and many hybrids of mostly perennial shrubs. Single, daisylike flowers, 2–4 in. (5–10 cm) wide with yellow or dark centers. Very narrow, smooth or lobed leaves, green above and silky white beneath. Plants grow 10–18 in. (25–45 cm) tall, 1 ft. (30 cm) wide.

Bloom color/season: Maroon, pink, red, bronze, orange, yellow, cream, white. Late spring and summer.

Plant hardiness: Zones 8–10.

Soil needs: Well-drained. 5.5–7.0 pH.

Planting: Full sun. 18 in. (45 cm) apart. Plant after frost.

Care: Water moderately. Divide when colonies develop central bare spots. Propagate from seeds, division, cuttings in spring and summer.

Features: Good choice for borders, containers, ground cover.

Common name: Geranium

Scientific name: *Pelargonium* species and *P.* × *hortorum*

Description: About 280 species of mostly perennial herbs and shrubs. Terminal clusters of 5-petaled, star-, saucer-, funnel-, butterfly-shaped flowers, 1–4 in. (25–100 mm) wide. Rounded, lobed, or ivylike, mid- to gray-green or multi-colored leaves to 5 in. (125 mm) wide. Plants grow to 4 ft. (1.2 m) tall.

Bloom color/season: White, pink, red, orange, purple, mauve. Spring–summer; some are everblooming.

Plant hardiness: Zones 7–10.

Soil needs: Average fertility, well-drained. 7.0–7.5 pH.

Planting: Full sun. 1 ft. (30 cm) apart. Plant in spring.

Care: Water moderately. Deadhead regularly. Cut back in winter. In cold-winter climates, store containers indoors. Propagate from seeds, division in spring.

Features: Good choice for borders, containers, cottage gardens, houseplants, massing. Mealybug, mildew, thrip susceptible.

Common name: Globeflower

Scientific name: *Trollius* species

Description: About 20 species of perennials. Brilliant, single, globe- or cup-shaped flowers 1–3 in. (25–75 mm) wide. Lobed or divided, dark green to bronze leaves. Plants grow 2–3 ft. (60–90 cm) tall, 18 in. (45 cm) wide. Bushy with flowering spikes.

Bloom color/season: Yellow, orange. Spring.

Plant hardiness: Zones 3–9.

Soil needs: Average fertility, moist, rich in organic matter. Mostly native to swampy locales. 7.0 pH.

Planting: Full sun to partial shade. 1 ft. (30 cm) apart. Plant in late summer.

Care: Easy. Water frequently; keep moist. Propagate from seeds, division.

Features: Good choice for accents, borders, massing, pond or stream shorelines. Disease and pest resistant.

Common name: Grass, Blue-eyed
Scientific name: *Sisyrinchium* species
Description: About 75 species of clumping perennials. Flat or rounded clusters of small, starlike flowers. Very narrow, grasslike, bluish green leaves 8–12 in. (20–30 cm) long. Plants grow 6–10 in. (15–25 cm) tall. Dainty, tufted with interesting texture.
Bloom color/season: Purple, blue; sometimes white, yellow. Spring–summer.
Plant hardiness: Zones 5–8. Avoid areas where ground freezes.
Soil needs: Moderate fertility, moist, well-drained. 7.0–8.0 pH.
Planting: Full sun to partial shade. 6 in. (15 cm) apart. Plant in late winter.
Care: Easy. Water regularly; slightly drought tolerant. Propagate from seeds, division in spring or autumn.
Features: Good choice for coastal gardens, color contrast in mixed beds, massing in place of traditional turfgrass. Western hemisphere native.

Common name: Grass, Eulalia
Scientific name: *Miscanthus sinensis*
Description: Graceful perennial grass. Flower panicles suitable for dried arrangements. Finely toothed, blue green and variegated leaves to 3 ft. (90 cm) long. Plants grow 5–10 ft. (1.5–3 m) tall. Large clumps.
Bloom color/season: Tan. Summer.
Plant hardiness: Zones 5–10.
Soil needs: Any well-drained. 7.0 pH.
Planting: Full sun to full shade. 5–6 ft. (1.5–1.8 m) apart. Plant in spring.
Care: Easy. Water moderately to abundantly. Cut back in winter. Propagate from seeds, division.
Features: Good choice for accent, backgrounds, large spaces, water feature shorelines, windbreak. Retain dry flowers on plants for interesting winter display. Has naturalized in some areas of the eastern United States.

Common name: Grass, Japanese Blood
Scientific name: *Miscanthus floridulus* 'Rubra'
Description: Non-blooming, colony-forming, ornamental grass. Interesting garden color and texture provided by striking, slender, upright, dark leaves, which emerge as green shoots and quickly turn red. Plants grow 1–2 ft. (30–60 cm) tall. Clumps.
Bloom color/season: Colorful red leaves. Spring–autumn.
Plant hardiness: Zones 7–10.
Soil needs: Average to rich fertility, moist, well-drained. 7.0 pH.
Planting: Full sun or light shade. 1–2 ft. (30–60 cm) apart. Plant in spring.
Care: Hardy. Water moderately. Clumps spread slowly. Dies back completely in winter. Propagate from division.
Features: Good choice for accents, borders, mixed beds, rock gardens, small spaces, water feature shorelines. Provides a striking ornamental grass when small stature is required by reduced scale.

Common name: Hollyhock

Scientific name: *Alcea* species

Description: Perhaps 60 species of biennials and perennials. Saucer-shaped flowers, 4 in. (10 cm) long. Flower spikes grow to 9 ft (3 m) tall; dwarf species are available. Round, rough-textured leaves 6–8 in (15–20 cm) wide radiate from the stalk's base. Stately.

Bloom color/season: Yellow, white, pink, red, maroon. Summer–autumn.

Plant hardiness: Zones 2–10.

Soil needs: Average fertility. Well-drained. 7.0–7.5 pH.

Planting: Full sun. 1 ft. (30 cm) apart. Sow seed in early summer; divide and transplant the following spring.

Care: Easy. Water regularly. Propagate from seeds, division.

Features: Good choice for accents, back of borders, center of beds, frame for benches, entrances. Rust, slug, snail susceptible.

Common name: Indigo, False

Scientific name: *Baptisia australis*

Description: Intensely colored, pea-shaped flowers 1 in. (25 mm) long. Clover-like bluish green leaves, turning black at first frost, 3 in. (75 mm) wide. Plants grow 3–6 ft. (90–180 cm) tall, 3–4 ft. (90–120 cm) wide. Lush, bushy.

Bloom color/season: Blue. Late spring–early summer.

Plant hardiness: Zones 3–9, dry areas.

Soil needs: Average to poor fertility, loam, well-drained. 6.5–7.0 pH.

Planting: Full sun to shade. 2–3 ft. (60–90 cm) apart. Plant in late autumn or early spring.

Care: Very easy. Water infrequently. Stake tallest plants. Propagate from seeds, division before or after flowering.

Features: Good choice for backgrounds, borders, cut flowers, hedges, massings, natural gardens. Slow growing but virtually indestructible. Powdery mildew, rust susceptible.

Common name: Iris, Bearded

Scientific name: *Iris* hybrids

Description: Thousands of varieties in three groups: tall, 2–4 ft. (60–120 cm) with showy flowers; medium, 1–2 ft. (30–60 cm) with large flowers; miniature or dwarf, 3–10 in. (75–250 mm). All have sword-shaped leaves, upright flowers.

Bloom color/season: Almost all colors, bicolor, blended. Spring–autumn.

Plant hardiness: Zones 5–10.

Soil needs: Rich fertility, moist, well-drained, rich in organic matter. 7.0–7.5 pH.

Planting: Full sun. 1–2 ft. (30–60 cm) apart. Avoid crowding. Summer–autumn.

Care: Moderately easy. Water thoroughly at planting, then regularly but infrequently. Apply low-nitrogen fertilizer in early spring and late summer. Avoid mulch and manure. Propagate from division of rhizome clumps after hottest summer days, at least every 3–4 years.

Features: Good choice for cut flowers. Many sweetly fragrant. Susceptible to a variety of pests, depending on region: iris borer, nematodes (south), bulb whitefly (west), verbena bud moth, iris weevil, thrip (north).

Common name: Knapweed
Scientific name: *Centaurea* species
Description: 400–500 species of annuals, biennials, and mainly perennials. Single or small clusters of fringed, tubular, thistlelike flowers 2–3 in. (50–75 mm) wide. Needlelike, deeply cut leaves 1 ft. (30 cm) long, gray green above and lighter beneath. Plants grow 1–3 ft. (30–90 cm) tall.
Bloom color/season: Lavender, pink, blue, yellow. Spring–summer.
Plant hardiness: Zones 4–9.
Soil needs: Average fertility, loam, well-drained. 5.0–6.5 pH.
Planting: Full sun to slight shade. 1–2 ft. (30–60 cm) apart. Plant in spring after last frost.
Care: Water moderately. Stake taller species. Propagate from seeds, division every 3–4 years.
Features: Good choice for backgrounds, cut flowers, foliage accent.

Common name: Lamb's-ears
Scientific name: *Stachys byzantina*
Description: Profuse clusters of flowers ½–1 in. (13–25 mm) wide on spikes 32 in. (80 cm) tall. Appealing lamb's ear-shaped, wrinkled, velvety, grayish to silvery white leaves 4–6 in. (10–15 cm) wide. Low, spreading foliage creates mounds of flowers.
Bloom color/season: Pink, purple. July–September.
Plant hardiness: Zones 4–10.
Soil needs: Average to poor fertility, dry, well-drained. 7.0 pH.
Planting: Full sun to partial shade. 10–18 in. (25–45 cm) apart. Plant in early spring.
Care: Moderately easy. Avoid overwatering. Propagate from division in early spring or early autumn.
Features: Good choice for borders, ground cover.

Common name: Lavender
Scientific name: *Lavandula* species
Description: About 20 species of aromatic perennial herbs and shrubs. Small, delicate flowers with blue, violet, or purple centers in dense clusters on slim cylindrical spikes. Needlelike, woolly, gray to gray green, semi-evergreen leaves 2 in. (50 mm) long. Plants grow 1–4 ft. (30–120 cm) tall. Upright, dense.
Bloom color/season: Blue to violet. Summer.
Plant hardiness: Zones 7–10.
Soil needs: Average to poor fertility, loam, well-drained. 6.5–7.5 pH.
Planting: Full sun. 12–18 in. (30–45 cm) apart. Plant after last frost.
Care: Water moderately. Mulch over winter in colder climates. Prune in spring to avoid straggliness. Propagate from division in early spring, cuttings in late summer.
Features: Good choice for borders, dried flowers, low hedges, rock gardens. Fragrant; dried flowers retain lavender scent for years and are a good choice for use in dried arrangements, sachets, soaps, and candles.

Common name: Lily
Scientific name: *Lilium* species
Description: Nearly 90 species of perennial bulbs. Single or double trumpet-, hanging-, bowl-, chalice-, reflexed-, or sunburst-shaped flowers with spotted centers on drooping stalks. Alternate or clustered leaves. Plants grow 2–8 ft. (60–245 cm) tall. Stately.
Bloom color/season: Most colors except blue. Spring–autumn.
Plant hardiness: Zones 3–10.
Soil needs: Rich fertility, sandy loam, moist, well-drained. 6.0 pH.
Planting: Full sun in cooler regions, elsewhere partial shade. 12–18 in. (30–45 cm) apart. Plant bulbs in autumn.
Care: Easy. Water regularly. Mulch with straw in winter. Use complete fertilizer lightly in early spring and again before bloom; avoid manure. Stake taller varieties during bloom. Propagate from bulbs, division in early autumn.
Features: Good choice for massing, mixed borders. Aphid, basal rot, botrytis blight, lily mosaic, lily virus, rodent susceptible.

Common name: Lily-of-the-Nile; African Lily
Scientific name: *Agapanthus orientalis*
Description: Dense clusters of 20–100 tube-shaped flowers, 8 in. (20 cm) wide. Sword-shaped, thick, succulent leaves. Plants grow 18–48 in. (45–120 cm) tall. Arching foliage, upright flower stems. Colonies may reach 3 ft. (90 cm) in diameter if undivided.
Bloom color/season: Bright blue, white. Summer.
Plant hardiness: Zones 8–11.
Soil needs: Average fertility, moist, well-drained. 6.0–7.0 pH.
Planting: Full sun to partial shade. 2 ft. (60 cm) apart.
Care: Easy. Water moderately. Feed liquid fertilizer. Propagate from seeds, division in autumn or spring.
Features: Good choice for beds, borders, containers, massing. Evergreen in mild-winter climates. Slow growing. Mealybug susceptible.

Common name: Lily, Peruvian
Scientific name: *Alstroemeria* species
Description: More than 50 species of herbaceous perennials. Clusters of 10–30 conspicuously colored, showy, delicate, trumpet-shaped flowers 2 in. (5 cm) long. Lance-shaped leaves 2 in. (50 mm) wide. Plants grow 18–60 in. (45–150 cm) tall.
Bloom color/season: Red, purple, yellow, bicolor. Spring–summer.
Plant hardiness: Zones 7–10. In colder zones, plant in spring; after bloom, lift and store indoors.
Soil needs: Rich fertility, moist, well-drained, rich in organic matter. 5.0–7.0 pH.
Planting: Full sun to partial shade. 1 ft. (30 cm) apart.
Care: Water regularly. Mulch or plant ground cover annuals to keep soil cool. Propagate from seeds, division of clumps in early spring or autumn. Avoid breaking brittle roots.
Features: Good choice for flower arrangements. Avoid cutting; gently pull stem from rhizome.

Common name: Lily, Plantain; Hosta

Scientific name: *Hosta* species

Description: About 40 species of herbaceous perennials. Sometimes drooping clusters of 6–10 lilylike, tubular-shaped flowers 1½ in. (38 mm) long. Lush, overlapping, lance-, heart-, oval-, or round-shaped, smooth to puckered, green or gold leaves. Plants grow 8–36 in. (20–90 cm) tall, to 5 ft. (1.5 m) wide.

Bloom color/season: White, pale blue, purple. Summer.

Plant hardiness: Zones 3–10.

Soil needs: Rich to poor fertility, loam, moist, well-drained. Avoid wet winter soil. 5.0 pH.

Planting: Partial to full shade. 1–3 ft. (30–90 cm) apart. Plant in spring.

Care: Very easy. Water regularly. Mulch young plants in winter. Fertilize regularly. Propagate from division of clumps in spring.

Features: Good choice for ground cover. Some fragrant flowers. Grown for foliage. Crown rot, slug, snail susceptible.

Common name: Lily, Toad

Scientific name: *Tricyrtis* species

Description: Nearly 15 species of rhizomatous perennials. Single or clusters of small, unusually shaped flowers 1 in. (25 mm) wide. Alternate, broadly oval, shiny, fuzzy, dark green leaves. Plants grow 2–3 ft. (60–90 cm) tall. Upright, arching.

Bloom color/season: Spotted yellow, white, purplish. Summer–autumn.

Plant hardiness: Zones 4–9.

Soil needs: Rich fertility, well-drained, rich in organic matter. 5.0 pH.

Planting: Partial shade. 18–24 in. (45–60 cm) apart.

Care: Water regularly. Propagate from seeds, division.

Features: Good choice for containers, next to paths and entrances to show off the flowers, shade gardens. Long lived. In colder areas, dig up the rhizomes and store indoors in winter.

Common name: Lilyturf

Scientific name: *Liriope* species

Description: About 5 species of evergreen perennials. Ten or more clusters of 4–7 flowers ⅙–¼ in. (1.6–6-mm) wide on somewhat pendulous or drooping stalks. Attractive, grasslike, glossy, sometimes variegated, evergreen leaves, 1½ in. (38 mm) wide, up to 2 ft. (60 cm) long. Plants grow 8–24 in. (20–60 cm) tall. Dense clumps.

Bloom color/season: Purple, white. Summer.

Plant hardiness: Zones 6–10.

Soil needs: Average to rich fertility, well-drained. 7.0 pH.

Planting: Partial sun to full shade. 8–12 in. (20–30 cm) apart. Plant in spring.

Care: Very easy. Water regularly but moderately. Propagate from division of offsets in early spring.

Features: Good choice for borders, edgings, ground cover. Matted growth of colonies stabilize slopes from erosion. Invasive in warm-winter climates. Slug, snail susceptible.

Common name: Lobelia
Scientific name: *Lobelia* species
Description: A diverse group of nearly 375 species. Bright, intensely colored flowers 1–1½ in. (25–38 mm) wide with drooping lips. Oblong to lance-shaped, medium to dark green leaves. Plants grow 2–4 ft. (60–120 cm) tall, 12–18 in. (30–45 cm) wide. Tall, stiff, shrublike.
Bloom color/season: Red, pink, white, blue. Summer.
Plant hardiness: Zones 2–10.
Soil needs: Rich fertility, loam, moist, well-drained. 6.5–7.5 pH.
Planting: Partial shade. 1 ft. (30 cm) apart. Plant in spring.
Care: Moderately difficult. Water frequently. Mulch in summer and winter. Propagate from division.
Features: *L. dortmanna* good choice for water garden shorelines, *L. erinus* for edging, *L. spicata* for backgrounds. Attracts hummingbirds.

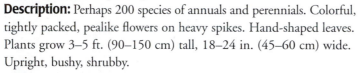

Common name: Lupine
Scientific name: *Lupinus* species
Description: Perhaps 200 species of annuals and perennials. Colorful, tightly packed, pealike flowers on heavy spikes. Hand-shaped leaves. Plants grow 3–5 ft. (90–150 cm) tall, 18–24 in. (45–60 cm) wide. Upright, bushy, shrubby.
Bloom color/season: Many colors and bicolors. Spring–summer.
Plant hardiness: Zones 3–8. Prefers cool nights.
Soil needs: Average to poor fertility, sandy or loam, moist, well-drained. 6.0–7.0 pH.
Planting: Full sun to partial shade. 18–24 in. (45–60 cm) apart. Plant in spring or late summer.
Care: Easy where summers are cooler. Water regularly. Mulch to keep cool. Fertilize once in spring and once in summer. Stake if necessary. Propagate from seeds, division, cuttings with some crown or root attached in early spring.
Features: Good choice for massing, mixed borders. Hybrids produce peppery odor. Aphid, crown rot, powdery mildew, rust susceptible.

Common name: Mallow
Scientific name: *Sidalcea* species
Description: About 20 species of perennials are cultivated. Small flowers with delicately fringed petals. Rounded, lobed leaves. Plants grow 2–4 ft. (60–120 cm) tall. Erect, stately.
Bloom color/season: Pale to deep pink. Summer.
Plant hardiness: Zones 5–9.
Soil needs: Loam, moist, well-drained. 7.0 pH.
Planting: Full sun to partial shade. 18–24 in. (45–60 cm) apart. Plant in autumn or early spring.
Care: Water regularly. Stake taller varieties. Propagate from seeds, division.
Features: Good choice for accents, borders, massing in meadows, mixed beds, prairie gardens. Western North American native.

Common name: Mallow, Rose
Scientific name: *Hibiscus Moscheutos*
Description: Single, dramatic, funnel-shaped flowers 5–12 in. (13–30 cm) wide usually with crimson centers on downy, canelike stems. Bold, lance-shaped to oval, toothed, hairy leaves to 8 in. (20 cm) long, green above and whitish beneath. Plants grow 5–8 ft. (1.5–2.4 m) tall, 24–30 in. (60–75 cm) wide. Erect and slightly spreading.
Bloom color/season: Red, white, pink, bicolor. Summer–autumn.
Plant hardiness: Zones 5–9.
Soil needs: Average fertility, well-drained to wetland. 7.0 pH.
Planting: Full sun to partial shade. 24–30 in. (60–75 cm) apart.
Care: Easy. Water abundantly. Fertilize regularly. Propagate from seeds, division.
Features: Good choice for backgrounds, fences, natural gardens, water feature shorelines. Aphid, blight, canker, Japanese beetle, leaf spot, rust, scale, whitefly susceptible.

Common name: Marguerite, Golden
Scientific name: *Anthemis tinctoria*
Description: Profuse masses of daisylike, upturned flowers 1½–2 in. (38–50 mm) wide. Neat, fernlike, finely cut, smooth leaves to 3 in. (8 cm) long, green above and felt gray beneath. Plants grow 2–3 ft. (60–90 cm) tall, 2–3 ft. (60–90 cm) wide. Dense, rounded shrub.
Bloom color/season: Golden yellow. Summer–early autumn.
Plant hardiness: Zones 3–10.
Soil needs: Poor fertility, dry, well-drained. Avoid heavy, wet, clay soil. 7.0 pH.
Planting: Full sun. 15–18 in. (38–45 cm) apart. Plant in late spring or early summer.
Care: Easy. Water infrequently. Deadhead flowers for continued bloom. Propagate from seeds, division every 1–2 years, stem cuttings in summer.
Features: Good choice for borders, cottage gardens, cut flowers. Fragrant. Flowers yield a yellow dye. Evergreen in warm climates.

Common name: Marigold, Marsh; Cowslip; Meadow-bright
Scientific name: *Caltha palustris*
Description: Double flowers 2 in. (50 mm) wide on each stem. Rounded to heart-shaped, toothed, bright green leaves to 7 in. (18 cm) wide. Plants grow 1–3 ft. (30–90 cm) tall, 1–2 ft. (30–60 cm) wide.
Bloom color/season: Yellow. Spring.
Plant hardiness: Zones 5–7.
Soil needs: Rich fertility, wet, soggy. 7.0 pH.
Planting: Full sun to partial shade. 1–2 ft. (30–60 cm) apart. Plant seeds in late summer.
Care: Keep wet. Propagate from seeds, division.
Features: Good choice for water feature with still water.

> **Warning**
>
> All parts of marsh marigold may cause skin irritation in sensitive individuals.

Common name: Masterwort
Scientific name: *Astrantia major*
Description: Colorful, showy flowers 2–3 in. (50–75 mm) wide with purplish centers. Palm-shaped, lobed, sometimes variegated leaves. Plants grow 2–3 ft. (60–90 cm) tall.
Bloom color/season: Creamy white, tinged pink by collar of purple bracts below the petals. Late spring.
Plant hardiness: Zones 5–7.
Soil needs: Average fertility, moist, well-drained. 7.0 pH.
Planting: Full sun to partial shade. 18 in. (45 cm) apart. Plant in autumn or early spring.
Care: Easy. Water frequently. Propagate from seeds in autumn, division in autumn or spring.
Features: Good choice for water feature.

Common name: Milkweed; Butterfly Weed
Scientific name: *Asclepias tuberosa*

> **Warning**
>
> Leaves and stems of milkweed are toxic if ingested. Avoid planting in areas frequented by children and pets.

Description: Dense, broad, flattened clusters of starlike, showy, vibrant flowers ⅓ in. (9 mm) wide with light-colored centers. Spiral or clusters of lance-shaped leaves to 4½ in. (11 cm) long. Plants grow 2–3 ft. (60–90 cm) tall, 12–18 in. (30–45 cm) wide. Stout, good texture, attractive.
Bloom color/season: Orange, yellow, red. Summer.
Plant hardiness: Zones 3–9.
Soil needs: Poor fertility, light, sandy, dry, well-drained. 7.0 pH.
Planting: Full sun. 12–18 in. (30–45 cm) apart. Plant in autumn or early spring.
Care: Easy. Water rarely, moderately in drought. Propagate from seeds.
Features: Good choice for borders, cut flowers, drought-tolerant, natural gardens. Attracts butterflies. Some varieties are invasive.

Common name: Mist Flower; Hardy Ageratum
Scientific name: *Eupatorium coelestinum*
Description: Showy, broad, open, flat-topped, dome-shaped, fluffy, dense clusters of 35–70 tubular, fuzzy flowers ½ in. (13 mm) wide. Opposite or clustered, triangular to oval, toothed, coarse, sometimes hairy leaves. Plants grow 1–3 ft. (30–90 cm) tall.
Bloom color/season: Blue, violet. Summer–autumn.
Plant hardiness: Zones 6–10.
Soil needs: Moist, loam, well-drained. Avoid soggy soil in winter. 7.0 pH.
Planting: Full sun to partial shade. 18–24 in. (45–60 cm) apart.
Care: Easy. Water regularly. Propagate from division in spring.
Features: Good choice for cut flowers, mixed borders. Attracts butterflies.

Common name: Monkshood; Aconite

Scientific name: *Aconitum Napellus*

Description: Double, dense clusters of helmet-shaped flowers 1–2 in. (25–50-mm) wide with visorlike extensions. Toothed, dark green leaves 2–4 in. (50–100 mm) wide. Plants grow to 3 ft. (90 cm) tall. Erect.

Bloom color/season: Blue, violet. Summer–autumn.

Plant hardiness: Zones 3–9.

Soil needs: Rich fertility, moist, well-drained. 5.0–6.0 pH.

Planting: Partial shade. 18 in. (45 cm) apart. Plant in autumn.

Care: Water regularly. Mulch the first winter in coldest regions. Stake taller plants. Propagate from seeds, division every 3–5 years.

Features: Good choice for back of beds.

> **Warning**
>
> All parts of monkshood are fatally toxic if ingested. Avoid planting in any area frequented by children and pets.

Common name: Morning Glory

Scientific name: *Convolvulus mauritanicus*

Description: Clusters of 1–6 bell-shaped flowers 1–2 in. (25–50 mm) wide with blue or violet centers. Round to oval, softly hairy, gray green leaves 1 in. (25 mm) long. Plants grow to 3 ft. (90 cm) tall. Loose and spreading.

Bloom color/season: Lavender blue. Late spring–summer.

Plant hardiness: Zones 7–10.

Soil needs: Tolerates dry soil, slow-drained. 6.0–8.0 pH.

Planting: Full sun to partial shade. 3 ft. (90 cm) apart. Plant in spring.

Care: Easy. Water moderately. Cut back in late winter or early spring. Propagate from seeds, division, cuttings. Can be invasive.

Features: Good choice for containers, ground cover. Blooms in early morning, sometimes closing by noon when conditions are overcast.

Common name: Navelwort

Scientific name: *Omphalodes* species

Description: About 24 species of perennials; six are cultivated for gardens. Sprays of flowers ½ in. (13 mm) wide. Simple, alternate, oval, fine, hairy leaves 1–3 in. (25–75 mm) long. Plants grow to 8 in. (20 cm) tall. Trailing.

Bloom color/season: Blue, white. Spring.

Plant hardiness: Zones 6–9.

Soil needs: Moderate fertility, moist, well-drained. 7.0 pH.

Planting: Partial to full shade. 1 ft. (30 cm) apart. Plant in spring.

Care: Water moderately. Propagate from seeds, division in early spring.

Features: Good choice for accent around bird baths and other garden accessories, ground cover, massing in meadows, prairies. Evergreen in warm climates.

Common name: Obedience Plant; False Dragonhead
Scientific name: *Physostegia virginiana*
Description: Dense clusters of irregular, opened-mouthed flowers 1 in. (25 mm) long with rose purple centers on tapering spikes. Opposite, neat, lance-shaped, toothed, green-and-white variegated leaves to 5 in. (13 cm) long. Plants grow to 4 ft. (1.2 m). Slender, erect.
Bloom color/season: Pink, white. Summer–early autumn.
Plant hardiness: Zones 2–9.
Soil needs: Rich fertility, loam, moist. 6.0 pH.
Planting: Full sun to partial shade. 1–2 ft. (30–60 cm) apart. Plant in spring and autumn.
Care: Very easy. Water regularly. Pinch to control lankiness. Propagate from division every 2–3 years in early spring.
Features: Good choice for borders. Flower holds its new place when pushed out of position, thus "obedient." Can become invasive.

Common name: Onion, Ornamental
Scientific name: *Allium* species
Description: More than 400 species of perennial bulbs. Unusual clusters 3–12 in. (75–300 mm) wide of tiny globelike flowers. Linear, aromatic, hollow, bright green leaves 1–3 ft. (30–90 cm) long. Plants grow 18–60 in. (45–150 cm) tall. Stiff.
Bloom color/season: Blue, purple, pink, white. Spring–autumn.
Plant hardiness: Zones 3–10.
Soil needs: Rich fertility. 7.0 pH.
Planting: Plant at depth equal to three times the height of the bulb, 1–4 in. (25–100 mm) apart. Plant in autumn.
Care: Very easy. Water abundantly. Propagate from small bulbs, offsets.
Features: Good choice for borders, food, natural gardens. Downy mildew, neck rot, onion maggot, onion smut, onion thrip, pink root susceptible.

Common name: Peony
Scientific name: *Paeonia* hybrids
Description: Depending on species and variety, single, semidouble, or double, showy flowers 3–10 in. (75–250 mm) wide. Large, medium texture, deeply lobed, glossy, green leaves. Plants grow 18–60 in. (45–150 cm) tall, 3 ft. (90 cm) wide. Rounded, bushy, stout to coarse.
Bloom color/season: Pink, white, red, yellow. Late spring–early summer.
Plant hardiness: Zones 3–8. Requires winter cold.
Soil needs: Rich fertility, loam, well-drained. 6.0 pH.
Planting: Full sun to partial shade. 2–4 ft. (60–120 cm) apart. Plant in late summer or autumn.
Care: Very easy. Water regularly. Mulch the first winter and in hot climates during summer. Fertilize at planting time and in spring. Stake taller varieties before buds break. Propagate from division in late summer or autumn.
Features: Good choice for borders, cut flowers. Some fragrant. Very long lived. Ant, botrytis, phytophthora blight, slug, snail susceptible.

Common name: Phlox, Garden; Perennial Phlox
Scientific name: *Phlox paniculata*
Description: Pyramid-shaped clusters 10–14 in. (25–36 cm) wide of small flowers. Thin, veiny, oval- to lance-shaped, dense, dark green leaves 3–6 in. (75–150 mm) long. Plants grow 1–2 ft. (30–60 cm) tall, 2 ft. (60 cm) wide.
Bloom color/season: White, pink, red, lavender, blue. Spring–summer.
Plant hardiness: Zones 3–10.
Soil needs: Rich fertility, moist, well-drained. 7.0 pH.
Planting: Full sun to partial shade. 18 in. (45 cm) apart. Plant in spring.
Care: Moderately difficult. Water frequently. Fertilize regularly. Stake for support. Propagate from seeds, division, cuttings.
Features: Good choice for borders. Some slightly fragrant. Powdery mildew, rust, spider mite susceptible.

Common name: Pincushion Flower
Scientific name: *Scabiosa caucasica*
Description: Clusters of delicate, frilly-petaled flowers 2–3 in. (50–75 mm) wide with circular, pincushion-like gray centers. Narrow, toothed, medium green leaves to 5 in. (13 cm) long. Plants grow 18–30 in. (45–75 cm) tall, 12–18 in. (30–45 cm) wide. Restrained.
Bloom color/season: Blue, white. Summer.
Plant hardiness: Zones 3–7.
Soil needs: Sandy or loam, moist, well-drained. Avoid very dry or soggy soil. 7.0–8.0 pH.
Planting: Full sun to partial shade. Prefers moist air. 12–15 in. (30–38 cm) apart. Plant in early spring.
Care: Moderately easy. Water regularly. Mulch in summer and in cold-climate winters. Propagate from division every 3–4 years in spring.
Features: Good choice for borders, cut flowers. Mildew, root rot susceptible.

Common name: Pinks
Scientific name: *Dianthus* species
Description: About 300 species of annuals, biennials, and perennials. Showy single or double, lacy flowers 1–1½ in. (25–38 mm) wide. Opposite, narrow, grasslike, mostly gray green evergreen leaves. Plants grow 1 ft. (30 cm) tall, 12–15 in. (30–38 cm) wide. Small, tufted, compact.
Bloom color/season: Bright pink, rose, white; occasionally yellow, bicolor. Spring–summer.
Plant hardiness: Zones 4–9.
Soil needs: Sandy, well-drained, rich in organic matter. Avoid damp soil in winter. 7.0–8.0 pH.
Planting: Full sun. 12–15 in. (30–38 cm) apart. Plant in late summer or autumn, early spring in colder regions.
Care: Easy. Water moderately. Mulch. Lightly protect in very cold winter. Propagate from seeds, division, layering, stem or shoot cuttings.
Features: Good choice for borders, edgings, rock gardens, walls. Pungent fragrance. Rust, wilt disease susceptible.

Common name: Plumbago, Dwarf
Scientific name: *Ceratostigma plumbaginoides*
Description: Single or clusters of brilliant flowers 3–4 in. (75–100 mm) wide with dark blue centers. Lush, oval, shiny, medium to fine-textured deep green leaves turning reddish bronze in autumn. Plants grow 12–20 in. (30–50 cm) tall, 18–24 in. (45–60 cm) wide. Low.
Bloom color/season: Blue. Summer–early autumn.
Plant hardiness: Zones 6–9.
Soil needs: Average fertility, loam, well-drained. Avoid very dry or soggy soil. 7.0 pH.
Planting: Full sun to partial shade. 12–18 in. (30–45 cm) apart. Plant in spring.
Care: Easy. Propagate from division every 2–4 years in spring, cuttings in early summer.
Features: Good choice for beds, edging, foreground, ground cover. Roots can be invasive, avoid planting near tree roots.

Common name: Poppy, Oriental
Scientific name: *Papaver orientale*
Description: Single or sometimes double, conspicuous, tissue-thin, bowl-shaped flowers 4–10 in. (10–25 cm) wide with black, silky centers. Large, toothed, coarse, hairy, light green to grayish leaves. Plants grow 2–4 ft. (60–120 cm) tall, 3 ft. (90 cm) wide. Wiry.
Bloom color/season: White, pink, dark red, orange. Late spring.
Plant hardiness: Zones 3–7. Short-lived in regions of warm winters.
Soil needs: Average to rich fertility, light or heavy, well-drained. 7.0 pH.
Planting: Full sun to partial shade. 15–20 in. (38–50 cm) apart. Plant in late summer–early autumn.
Care: Moderately easy. Water regularly. Mulch in first winter and in summer to keep cool. Propagate from division every 4–5 years in late summer.
Features: Good choice for cut flowers. Long lived. Aphid, bacterial blight, downy mildew, northern root-knot nematode susceptible.

Common name: Primrose, English
Scientific name: *Primula vulgaris* and *P.* × *polyantha*
Description: Single or small clusters of vividly colored small flowers. Paddle-shaped, toothed, wrinkled, bright green leaves to 10 in. (25 cm) long. Plants grow 6–9 in. (15–23 cm) tall, 6–15 in. (15–38 cm) wide. Low.
Bloom color/season: Yellow, purple, blue. Late winter–summer.
Plant hardiness: Zones 6–8.
Soil needs: Rich fertility, moist. 6.0–7.5 pH.
Planting: Partial to full shade. 6–15 in. (15–38 cm) apart. Plant in spring or late autumn.
Care: Moderately easy. Water regularly, especially during drought. Mulch in winter. Propagate from seeds, division every 3–4 years after flowering.
Features: Good choice for massing, moist areas, rock gardens. Lightly fragrant. Bacterial leaf spot, fungus leaf spot, nematode, root rot, slug, snail susceptible.

Common name: Primrose, Evening; Sundrop
Scientific name: *Oenothera* species
Description: About 80 species of mostly perennials. Showy, broad, silky petals on saucer-shaped flowers up to 5 in. (13 cm) wide. Sundrop blooms in daytime; evening primrose at night. Linear, lobed, or toothed leaves. Plants grow 6–24 in. (15–60 cm) tall, 2 ft. (60 cm) wide. Spreading.
Bloom color/season: Yellow, pink, white. Summer.
Plant hardiness: Zones 4–9.
Soil needs: Loam, well-drained. 7.0 pH.
Planting: Full sun. 18–24 in. (45–60 cm) apart. Plant seeds in spring or early summer.
Care: Very easy. Water moderately. Fertilize soil with well-rotted manure before planting. Can become weedy. Propagate from seeds, division in autumn or early spring.
Features: Good choice for evening gardens, slopes. Very fragrant.

Common name: Queen-of-the-Prairie
Scientific name: *Filipendula rubra*
Description: Clusters of fluffy flower plumes. Lush, toothed, fine-textured leaves 4–8 in. (10–20 cm) wide, green above and paler beneath. Plants grow to 8 ft. (2.4 m) tall, 1–2 ft. (30–60 cm) wide. Feathery, restrained.
Bloom color/season: White, pink, deep red, purple. Spring–summer.
Plant hardiness: Zones 3–9.
Soil needs: Rich fertility, loam, moist to soggy. Poor in desert or arid conditions. 7.0 pH.
Planting: Full sun to partial shade. 1–2 ft. (30–60 cm) apart. Plant in spring.
Care: Moderately easy. Water abundantly. Fertilize regularly. Propagate from seeds, division in early spring.
Features: Good choice for backgrounds, natural gardens. Long-lasting blooms. Naturalized in North American midwest.

Common name: Red-Hot Poker; Poker Plant; Torch-Lily
Scientific name: *Kniphofia* species
Description: About 70 species of rhizomatous perennials. Very conspicuous clusters 4–6 in. (10–15 cm) long of brilliant, tubular flowers 1 in. (25 mm) long atop stiff, bare spikes. Broad, grasslike, stiff-textured, gray green leaves up to 3 ft. (90 cm) long. Plants grow 1–5 ft. (30–150 cm) tall, 36–42 in. (90–105 cm) wide. Stout.
Bloom color/season: Red, yellow, orange, cream. Late spring–autumn.
Plant hardiness: Zones 5–10.
Soil needs: Sandy, well-drained. Avoid soggy soil. 7.0 pH.
Planting: Full sun. 18 in. (45 cm) apart. Plant in early spring.
Care: Withhold water in dry season. Protect or lift and store indoors in winter. Propagate from seeds, division, offsets in early spring.
Features: Good choice for bold accent in mixed borders, tropical gardens. Evergreen in mild climates. Attracts hummingbirds.

Common name: Rose, Lenten; Hellebore
Scientific name: *Helleborus orientalis*
Description: Cup- or bell-shaped flowers 3 in. (75 mm) wide with dark centers nodding on a pendulous stalk. Hand-shaped, lobed, broad, glossy, often evergreen leaves to 16 in. (40 cm) wide. Plants grow 18 in. (45 cm) tall. Dense clumps.
Bloom color/season: Cream, pink fading to maroon, brown. Late autumn and early spring.
Plant hardiness: Zones 4–5.
Soil needs: Rich fertility, moist, well-drained. 6.5 pH.
Planting: Partial to full shade. 1–2 ft. (30–60 cm) apart.
Care: Moderately difficult. Keep moist. Mulch summer and winter. Fertilize 12 times a year. Propagate from seeds in early summer, division of rhizomes in late summer.
Features: Good choice under canopy of deciduous trees or other moist, shady spot with rich soil. Leaf spot susceptible.

> **Warning**
>
> Roots are toxic if ingested. Avoid planting in areas frequented by children and pets.

Common name: Sage
Scientific name: *Salvia* species
Description: More than 750 species of perennial herbs and shrubs. Diverse family group with plants of many forms. Single, two-lipped, hooded flowers 1 in. (25 mm) wide on slender stalks. Opposite, dense, sometimes toothed, medium-textured, gray green leaves. Plants grow 1–3 ft. (30–90 cm) tall, 1–2 ft. (30–60 cm) wide.
Bloom color/season: Blue, purple, white, red. Spring–autumn.
Plant hardiness: Zones 4–10, especially the southern U.S.
Soil needs: Average to poor fertility, loam, dry, well-drained. 6.0–7.5 pH.
Planting: Full sun. 10–24 in. (25–60 cm) apart. Plant in early spring.
Care: Easy. Water moderately, drought tolerant once established. Protect in cold winters. Propagate from seeds, division, cuttings.
Features: Good choice for dry sites, mixed borders, rock gardens. Very fragrant. Leaf spot, rust, scale, whitefly susceptible.

Common name: Sage, Russian
Scientific name: *Perovskia* species
Description: About seven species of herbaceous perennials. Clusters of soft, small, tubular, two-lipped flowers on tall, woody stems. Soft, silvery gray leaves. Plants grow 3–4 ft. (90–120 cm) tall. Delicate, massing, spreading.
Bloom color/season: Lavender blue. Late spring–summer.
Plant hardiness: Zones 3–7.
Soil needs: Average fertility, loam, well-drained. 7.0 pH.
Planting: Full sun. Average soil. 2–3 ft. (60–90 cm) apart.
Care: Hardy. Water moderately. Propagate from seeds, summer cuttings of young wood.
Features: Good choice for accent to garden accessories, borders, filler, massing, summer hedge, windbreak. Fragrant. Long-lasting blooms.

Common name: Solomon's-seal

Scientific name: *Polygonatum* species

Description: About 30 species of rhizomatous perennials. Single or clusters of nodding, bell-shaped flowers ½ in. (13 mm) long in two rows on arching stems. Alternate, rich green to bluish green leaves up to 7 in. (18 cm) long. Plants grow 2–4 ft. (60–120 cm) tall, 18–36 in. (45–90 cm) wide. Graceful, arching to erect.

Bloom color/season: Green, yellow, white. Spring.

Plant hardiness: Zones 3–9.

Soil needs: Rich fertility, loam, moist. 5.0 pH.

Planting: Partial to full shade. 18–36 in. (45–90 cm) apart.

Care: Moderately easy. Water regularly. Mulch during summer. Propagate from division.

Features: Good choice with shade-loving shrubs, spring-flowering bulbs, natural gardens. Use foliage in arrangements.

Common name: Speedwell

Scientific name: *Veronica* species

Description: About 250 species of annuals and perennials. Dense spires of tiny flowers. Lance-shaped, medium-textured, light green to grayish leaves, 2 in. (50 mm) long. Plants grow 1–2 ft. (30–60 cm) tall, 12–18 in. (30–45 cm) wide. Bushy.

Bloom color/season: Blue, pink, white. Late spring–summer.

Plant hardiness: Zones 3–8.

Soil needs: Average to poor fertility, loam, well-drained. 7.0 pH.

Planting: Full sun to partial shade. 1–2 ft. (30–60 cm) apart. Plant in spring or autumn.

Care: Moderately easy. Water regularly. Propagate from seeds, division in spring or autumn, cuttings.

Features: Good choice for borders, rock gardens. Downy mildew, leaf spot susceptible.

Common name: Spirea, False; Meadow Sweet

Scientific name: *Astilbe* species

Description: About 14 species of herbaceous perennials. Quantities of tiny flowers produce dramatic, fluffy plumes. Neatly formed, fernlike, compound, glossy, dark green leaves. Plants grow 8–42 in. (20–105 cm) tall, 1–2 ft. (30–60 cm) wide. Feathery.

Bloom color/season: White, pink, red, purple. Summer.

Plant hardiness: Zones 4–10.

Soil needs: Rich fertility, moist. 7.0 pH.

Planting: Partial to full shade. 1–2 ft. (30–60 cm) apart. Plant in spring.

Care: Moderately easy. Water and mulch frequently. Fertilize in spring as growth begins. Propagate from seeds, division.

Features: Good choice for border filler, containers, ground cover, near water feature. Leave dried flower spikes on plants through winter for ornamental effect. Powdery mildew, Japanese beetle, slug, snail susceptible.

Common name: Spurge
Scientific name: *Euphorbia* species

Description: More than 1600 species of herbaceous perennials, shrubs, and trees. Conspicuous, highly colored flowers. Oblong, medium-textured dark green leaves, turning dark red in autumn. Many succulent, cactuslike species. Plants grow 1 ft. (30 cm) tall. Neat, mounded, symmetrical, bushy.
Bloom color/season: Yellow. Spring.
Plant hardiness: Zones 5–9.
Soil needs: Average to poor fertility, dry, well-drained. 6.0–7.0 pH.
Planting: Full sun to partial shade. 12–15 in. (30–38 cm) apart. Plant in spring.
Care: Easy. Water moderately. Propagate from seeds, division in spring or autumn, cuttings.
Features: Succulent species are good choice for borders, accents. *E. pulcherrima* is the popular holiday poinsettia. Avoid use near water features; the sap of most species is toxic to fish.

> **Warning**
>
> Sap of cushion spurge may cause contact dermatitis similar to poison oak, ivy, and sumac in susceptible individuals.

Common name: Statice; Sea Lavender
Scientific name: *Limonium latifolium*
Description: Large, cloudlike, pyramidal, loosely branched clusters of small, lacy flowers with blue violet centers. Oblong to elliptical, hairy leaves 10 in. (25 cm) long. Plants grow 30 in. (75 cm) tall, 3 ft. (90 cm) wide. Airy, graceful.
Bloom color/season: Lavender blue to violet. Summer.
Plant hardiness: Zones 3–10, especially good near coasts.
Soil needs: Average to poor fertility, well-drained. Can be grown in salty marshes. 6.0 pH.
Planting: Full sun. 18 in. (45 cm) apart.
Care: Moderately difficult. Drought tolerant once established. Stake if branches are weak. Propagate from seeds, division in early spring or late autumn.
Features: Good choice for borders, cut flowers, drying, near water features. Long-lasting blooms.

Common name: Stonecrop; Orpine
Scientific name: *Sedum* species
Description: Perhaps 600 species of succulent perennials. Diverse group of plants. Dense, flat clusters resembling broccoli with small, showy, star-shaped flowers 3–4 in. (8–10 cm) wide. Alternate and overlapping, succulent, thick-textured, bright-, blue-, or reddish-green leaves to 3 in. (75 mm) wide. Plants grow 3–12 in. (75–300 mm) tall, 1 ft. (30 cm) wide. Low, mounded.
Bloom color/season: White, yellow, pink, red, purple. May–October.
Plant hardiness: Zones 3–10.
Soil needs: Sandy, well-drained. 6.0–7.5 pH.
Planting: Full sun to partial shade. 1–2 ft. (30–60 cm) apart. Plant in spring.
Care: Easy. Drought tolerant. Propagate from seeds, division, stem cuttings in spring.
Features: Good choice for containers, edging, ground covers, rock gardens. Attracts butterflies. Nearly or truly evergreen.

Common name: Strawberry, Wild
Scientific name: *Fragaria* species
Description: About 12 species of herbaceous perennials. Oval to cone-shaped, coarsely serrated leaves. Round, five-petaled flowers. Not a true berry, bears red seedlike clusters in autumn. Plants grow to 3 ft. (90 cm) tall.
Bloom color/season: White, pink, dull red. Summer–autumn.
Plant hardiness: Zones 3–10.
Soil needs: Sandy. 7.0 pH.
Planting: Full sun. 12–30 in. (30–75 cm) apart, depending on variety. Plant in early spring.
Care: Requires frequent care. Water frequently; do not let soil dry out. Protect in cold winters. Fertilize at planting and throughout season. Propagate from division of runners or plant clean, rooted plants in late summer.
Features: Good choice for accents, ground cover, massing. Fruit and flowers attract birds and butterflies. Disease and pest resistant.

Common name: Sunflower, Perennial
Scientific name: *Helianthus* species
Description: About 150 species of annuals and perennials. Single or double, round flowers 3–12 in. (75–300 mm) wide, with single or overlapping petals and dark centers. Large, alternate or opposite, usually coarsely toothed, coarse-textured leaves. Plants grow 3–7 ft. (90–210 mm) tall, 18–24 in. (45–60 cm) wide. Tall, engaging.
Bloom color/season: Yellow. Summer–autumn.
Plant hardiness: Zones 4–8.
Soil needs: Average fertility, moist, well-drained. 5.0–7.0 pH.
Planting: Full sun to partial shade. Good air circulation. 18–36 in. (45–90 cm) apart. Plant in spring.
Care: Easy. Water regularly but moderately. Fertilize occasionally. Stake tallest varieties. Propagate from seeds, division every 3–4 years in autumn or spring.
Features: Good choice for borders, cut flowers, massing. Powdery mildew, rust, sap-sucking plant insects, stalk borer, sunflower maggot, sunflower moth larvae susceptible.

Common name: Thistle, Globe
Scientific name: *Echinops* species
Description: About 100 species of herbaceous biennials and perennials. Dense, bristly, round clusters 2–3 in. (50–75 mm) wide of tubular, spiny flowers. Spiny, thistlelike, toothed, coarse-textured leaves, deep green above and usually white beneath. Plants grow 3–4 ft. (90–120 cm) tall, 18–24 in. (45–60 cm) wide. Stiff, erect, bold.
Bloom color/season: Blue, white. Summer.
Plant hardiness: Zones 4–8.
Soil needs: Average to rich fertility, loam, well-drained. Avoid soggy soil. 5.0 pH.
Planting: Full sun to partial shade. 18–24 in. (45–60 cm) apart. Plant seed in early spring.
Care: Moderately easy. Water moderately. Stake if soil is rich. Thin regularly. Propagate from seeds, root cuttings, division every 3–4 years in spring.
Features: Good choice for accents, back of beds, cut flowers, drying.

Common name: Thrift; Sea Pink
Scientific name: *Armeria maritima*
Description: Spherical clusters up to 5 in. (13 cm) wide of rounded flowers ½–1 in. (13–25 mm) wide on stiff stems. Narrow, linear, grasslike, evergreen leaves 4 in. (10 cm) long in tufts to 6 in. (15 cm) long. Plants grow 4–24 in. (10–60 cm) tall, 12–18 in. (30–45 cm) wide. Low, tufted.
Bloom color/season: White to deep rose pink. Spring–year around.
Plant hardiness: Zones 3–10.
Soil needs: Poor fertility, light, sandy, very well-drained. 7.0 pH.
Planting: Full sun. Moist. 8–12 in. (20–30 cm) apart. Plant in late spring or early summer.
Care: Very hardy. Water moderately. In very poor soil, lightly fertilize. Deadhead to neaten appearance after bloom. Propagate from seeds, division.
Features: Good choice for cut flowers, edging, ground cover, planting near seacoast, rock gardens. Clumps spread slowly. Flower is medicinal.

Common name: Tickseed; Coreopsis
Scientific name: *Coreopsis* species
Description: Over 100 species of annuals and perennials. Single or double, daisylike flowers 3 in. (8 cm) wide with yellow or purplish centers. Long, straplike, toothed or lobed leaves. Plants grow 6–36 in. (15–90 cm) tall, 1 ft. (30 cm) wide.
Bloom color/season: Orange yellow, brownish, rose, bicolor. Summer–autumn.
Plant hardiness: Zones 4–10.
Soil needs: Loam, well-drained. 5.0–6.0 pH.
Planting: Full sun. 12–18 in. (30–45 cm) apart. Plant in spring or summer.
Care: Very easy. Water occasionally during drought. Fertilize occasionally. Propagate from seeds, division in spring, cuttings in spring.
Features: Good choice for cut flowers, natural gardens. Rapid growth and spread. Deadhead to promote blooms. Long blooming season. Attractive foliage contrasts nicely with blooms and provides interesting texture. Leaf spot, rust, powdery mildew, chewing insects susceptible.

Common name: Tree Mallow
Scientific name: *Lavatera arborea*
Description: Single or loose clusters of cup-shaped flowers 3 in. (75 mm) wide. Soft-textures, rounded, 3–5 lobed, midgreen leaves, 3–9 in. (8–22 cm) in diameter. Grey, hairy stems. Plants grow to 3–10 ft. (1–3 m) tall, 6 ft. (1.8 m) wide.
Bloom color/season: Pink, purple. Summer.
Plant hardiness: Zones 6–9.
Soil needs: Moderate fertility, sandy, moist, well-drained. 7.0 pH.
Planting: Full sun. 3–6 ft. (90–180 cm) apart. Plant in spring.
Care: Easy. Water moderately. Propagate from seeds.
Features: Good choice for hedges, screens. *L. arborea* 'variegata' has attractive mottled leaves.

Common name: Trillium; Wake Robin
Scientific name: *Trillium* species
Description: About 30 species of herbaceous perennials. Showy flowers 3–6 in. (8–15 cm) wide with green centers. Broad, oval, wavy leaves up to 6 in. (15 cm) long. Plants grow 12–18 in. (30–45 cm) tall, 1 ft. (30 cm) wide. Low.
Bloom color/season: White fading to pink. Early spring.
Plant hardiness: Zones 5–9.
Soil needs: Rich fertility, constantly moist, rich in organic matter. 6.5–7.0 pH.
Planting: Partial to deep shade. 5–8 in. (13–20 cm) apart.
Care: Water regularly. Propagate from seeds, division.
Features: Good choice for natural gardens, water features, wooded areas. Dormant and inconspicuous during summer. Avoid collecting native plants for home gardens.

Common name: Twinspur
Scientific name: *Diascia Barberae*
Description: Flowers with distinctive, orchidlike blossoms, ½ in. (13 mm) long. Toothed, heart-shaped leaves, to 1½ in. (38 mm) long. Plants grow 10 in. (25 cm) tall, 1 ft. (30 cm) wide. Mat forming.
Bloom color/season: Rosy pink, apricot. Spring–autumn.
Plant hardiness: Zones 8–9.
Soil needs: Average fertility, moist, well-drained. 7.0 pH.
Planting: Full sun to partial shade. 15 in. (38 cm) apart. Plant in spring; autumn in southern U.S.
Care: Easy. Water in dry weather. Deadhead to prolong bloom. Propagate by seeds, cuttings.
Features: Good choice for containers, front of borders, ground cover, understory. Slug, snail susceptible.

Common name: Verbena
Scientific name: *Verbena* species
Description: About 200 species of annuals and perennials. Clusters of broad, flat flowers ½ in. (13 mm) wide on wiry stems. Opposite, oval, bluntly toothed, hairy leaves 4 in. (10 cm) long. Plants grow 8–18 in. (20–45 cm) tall. Creeping.
Bloom color/season: Pink, red, yellow, white, purple. Spring–frost.
Plant hardiness: Zones 6–9.
Soil needs: Rich fertility, well-drained. 7.0 pH.
Planting: Full sun. 1–2 ft. (30–60 cm) apart, depending on variety. Plant after frost.
Care: Avoid watering foliage. Propagate from division, cuttings in spring. Grow as annuals in cold-winter climates.
Features: Good choice for edging, rock gardens, tropical gardens. Some are a cultivar of the North American native known as vervain. Budworm, powdery mildew, verbena leaf miner, verbena yellow woolly-bear caterpillar susceptible.

Common name: Violet, Sweet
Scientific name: *Viola odorata*
Description: Single and double flat-headed flowers ¾ in. (19 mm) wide. Oval to kidney-shaped, toothed leaves. Plants grow 8–24 in. (20–60 cm) tall. Tufted.
Bloom color/season: Deep violet, rose. Early spring.
Plant hardiness: Zones 6–9. Avoid areas of long, hot, dry summer.
Soil needs: Rich fertility, loam, moist, well-drained. 5.5–6.5 pH.
Planting: Full sun to partial shade. 8–12 in. (20–30 cm) apart. Plant in late summer.
Care: Water regularly. Propagate from seeds, division.
Features: Good choice for edgings, planting near coasts. Fragrant. Spider mite susceptible. Can be invasive.

Common name: Yarrow
Scientific name: *Achillea* species
Description: Almost 100 species of aromatic perennial herbs. Large, flat-topped clusters of flowers 3–5 in. (75–125 mm) wide. Finely cut, soft-textured, green or gray green leaves. Plants grow 6–54 in. (15–135 cm) tall, 12–18 in. (30–45 cm) wide. Open and erect.
Bloom color/season: White, yellow, pink. Spring–year-round.
Plant hardiness: Zones 3–9.
Soil needs: Average to poor fertility, dry, well-drained. 7.0 pH.
Planting: Full sun. 1–2 ft. (30–60 cm) apart. Plant in spring, autumn.
Care: Very easy. Water moderately; very drought resistant. Propagate from division every 2–4 years in spring or early autumn, stem cuttings in midsummer.
Features: Good choice for borders, cut flowers, drying, massing for accent, rock gardens. Evergreen in warmer climates. Powdery mildew, stem rot susceptible.

Common name: Yucca; Adam's Needle
Scientific name: *Yucca filamentosa*
Description: Waxy, drooping flowers 2–3 in. (50–75 mm) wide. Conspicuous, stiffly upright, swordlike, evergreen, succulent leaves to 1 in. (25 mm) wide, 30 in. (75 cm) long, edged with pencil-thin filaments that peel back and hang loosely. Plants grow 3–10 ft. (90–300 cm) tall. Tall, stiff, pointed.
Bloom color/season: Creamy white. Summer.
Plant hardiness: Zones 4–10.
Soil needs: Well-drained. 6.0–7.5 pH.
Planting: Full sun. 3–10 ft (90–300 cm) apart. Plant in spring.
Care: Water regularly on an infrequent schedule; drought tolerant once established. Propagate from seeds, cuttings.
Features: Good choice for accents, arid, desert gardens. Foliage is sometimes used with dried seedpods and flower heads for arrangements. Flowers may be fragrant at night. Black aphid, leaf spot susceptible.

The United States Department of Agriculture [USDA] Plant Hardiness Zone Map provides a general guide to growing conditions in North America. It divides the continent into 11 zones based on the average minimum annual temperatures within each zone. This system has been adapted to other areas of the world [see Maps, pg. 116–117]. The zones roughly predict which plants will survive in a given area. Because weather varies from year to year, the actual minimum temperatures may be lower or higher than indicated on the plant hardiness map.

When you're planning a garden, use the information contained in the map to guide your plant selections. First find your locale on the map, then identify your zone by comparing its color to the legend. Many growers include zone information on their plant tags and seed packages for your convenience.

Climate and microclimate govern plant choices and when gardens are planned and planted

Remember, perennial plants grow best in zones where they've adapted fully to the climate. It's possible that plants from warmer hardiness zones than yours may live and bloom in your garden during a series of warm-winter years, only to fail when normal cold years are experienced again.

Plant Hardiness Around the World

Your major concern in addition to plant hardiness zone will be the first and last frost dates in your area [see Approximate Frost-free Dates, pg. 116]. Sow seed indoors for cold-season plants—those that tolerate soil temperatures for germination of 40–50°F (4–10°C)—six weeks before the last frost. Wait a few more weeks for warm-season plants—those that prefer planting temperatures of 60°F (16°C) or higher. The average first and last frost dates for your area are general guidelines, however, and should be used subject to experience and advice.

Moreover, neither zone maps nor frost charts can account for the effects of thermal belts, nearby bodies of water, topography, and other factors that create microclimates within zones. Only careful observation will give you an accurate picture of climatic conditions in your own backyard.

USDA Plant Hardiness Around the World
North America

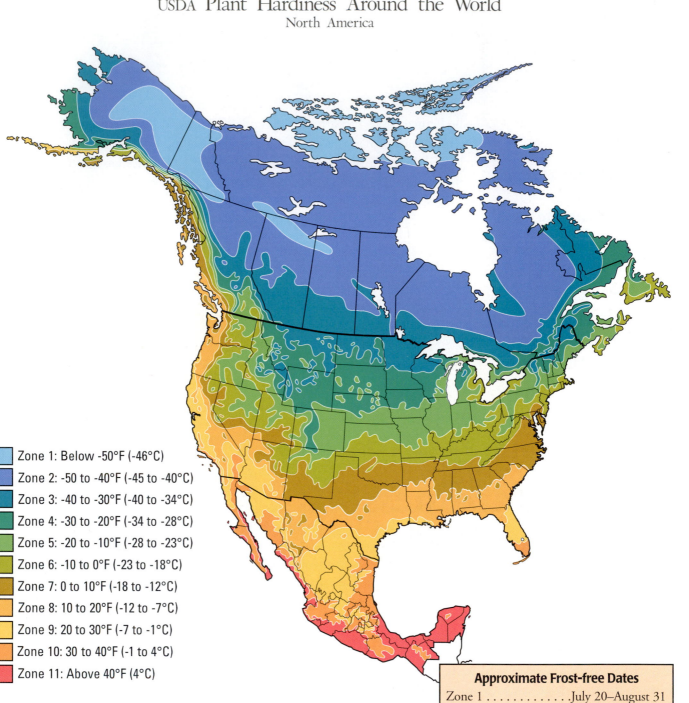

Zone 1: Below -50°F (-46°C)
Zone 2: -50 to -40°F (-45 to -40°C)
Zone 3: -40 to -30°F (-40 to -34°C)
Zone 4: -30 to -20°F (-34 to -28°C)
Zone 5: -20 to -10°F (-28 to -23°C)
Zone 6: -10 to 0°F (-23 to -18°C)
Zone 7: 0 to 10°F (-18 to -12°C)
Zone 8: 10 to 20°F (-12 to -7°C)
Zone 9: 20 to 30°F (-7 to -1°C)
Zone 10: 30 to 40°F (-1 to 4°C)
Zone 11: Above 40°F (4°C)

Approximate Frost-free Dates

Zone 1	July 20–August 31
Zone 2	July 10–September 10
Zone 3	June 30–September 15
Zone 4	June 15–September 25
Zone 5	May 25–October 10
Zone 6	May 15–October 20
Zone 7	April 25–November 1
Zone 8	April 15–November 10
Zone 9	March 15–November 15
Zone 10	February 10–December 10
Zone 11	Frost-free All Year

USDA Plant Hardiness Around the World
Australia

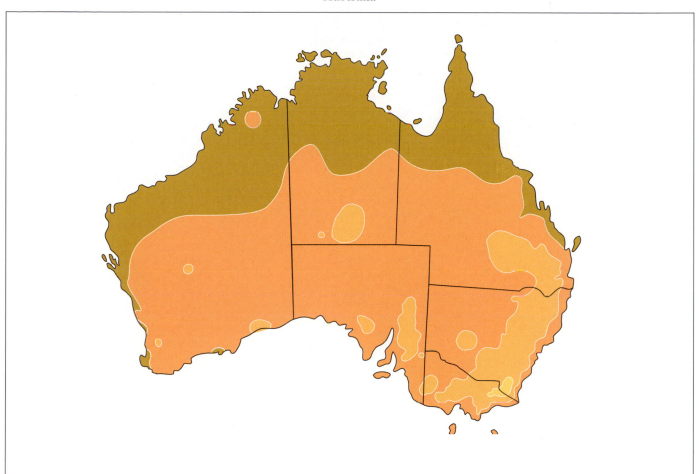

South Africa

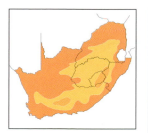

New Zealand

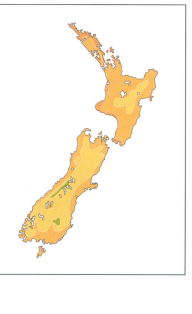

Europe

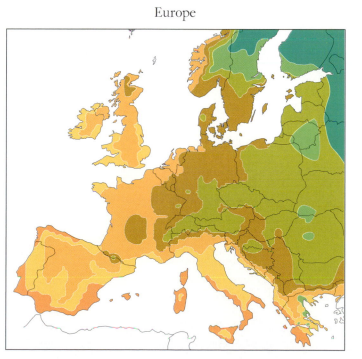

ON-LINE INDEX